For all of us that loved their first book, *Seen, Beyond the Spiral* is a must-read. Written by two experienced professionals, Will Hutcherson, and Dr. Chinwé Williams, this book is a comprehensive guide to help teens and young adults cope and thrive with anxiety. With practical tools, action steps, and a faith-based approach, this book offers hope and support to those in need. *Beyond the Spiral* provides a holistic approach to managing anxiety that will impact your life on multiple levels. If you or someone you know is struggling with anxiety, don't hesitate to grab this book today.

DR. KEVIN MONAHAN
Graduate Professor, Next Gen Ministry, Liberty University

Anxiety has always been a part of the human experience, but the level of anxiety people are now experiencing has never been higher. This is especially true of the emerging generation. The good news is that experts Dr. Chinwé Williams and Will Hutcherson have compiled an effective, easy-to-read, practical manual to help young people—and those of all ages—overcome anxiety. The book includes simple exercises that will lead to God's peace in the midst of the storms of life that come your way.

DR. ALAN EHLER
Southeastern University Professor, Pastor, and Author
of *How to Make Big Decisions Wisely* (Zondervan)

I will pay my kids to read this book. Finally, a book that provides clarity for teens and young adults about the worry and anxiety they feel. Dr. Chinwé and Will understand these emotions and provide hopeful steps to help develop skills to manage them.

CASEY ROSS
Pastor and Author of *Life & Faith: from "This is it!" to "This is it!"*

Beyond the Spiral by Will Hutcherson and Dr. Chinwé Williams is a game-changer for young people struggling with anxiety. This book provides many helpful strategies for breaking free from the negative thought patterns that can keep us trapped in an anxious mindset. Will and Chinwé offer a welcome message of hope for anyone seeking relief from worry and fear.

JON ACUFF
New York Times Bestselling author of
Soundtracks, the Surprising Solution to Overthinking

I have been waiting for a practical resource to help young people navigate panic, stress, and anxiety, and here it is. Most young people will see themselves in the pages of this book as it addresses anxiety's lies which lead to unhealthy responses. Will and Dr Chinwé provide easy-to-apply tools to confront the lies, understand what's true, take action, and invite God into the whole process. This book is a game changer.

ALLY EVANS
NextGen Leader, Life.Church

The genius of Will and Dr. Chinwé is that they put a "label" on the indescribable emotional trap of the "anxiety spiral" that so easily sucks in teenagers (and adults for that matter). Reading the "label" helps people to know what is contained within and then offers steps to help them find resolve, help, or peace! Brilliant words!

DR. KEVIN W. NORWOOD, DMIN, MAPT,
Student Pastor, Owasso First Assembly

This book is a must-read for teenagers and young adults. Dr. Chinwé and Will provide a needed perspective on anxiety, presenting the truth behind the lies we often tell ourselves and providing practical steps that empower readers to face anxiety head-on.

MATT MANNO
Nextgen Pastor, New Life Fellowship Church, NYC

In this day and age, teens and emerging adults are suffering from anxiety like never before, and the consequences are heartbreaking. Dr. Williams and Will have again combined faith and clinical principles to provide important steps for young people manage the tough moments in life.

DR. LAYLA J. BONNER, LMFT, NCC
Assistant Professor in the Master of Arts degree program
in Mental Health Counseling at Belmont University

I have been counseling kids and families for the past 30 years. And I have never seen anything take a toll on teenagers and young adults the way anxiety has in the past few years. It lies to them, robs them of their confidence and ultimately steals their hope . . . hope in who they are and hope in the future God has prepared for them. It's time for it to stop. We need voices who are speaking thoughtful, practical, hope-filled truth into the darkness of this anxiety-ridden world. Dr. Chinwé Williams and Will Hutcherson are two such voices. Chinwé is not only a dear friend, but one of the people I trust most in the mental health profession. In *Beyond the Spiral*, Dr. Chinwé and Will offer evidence-based strategies kids and young adults who are facing anxiety can start to use today. But they don't stop there. They speak truth into the lies that anxiety tells us. And, even more importantly, they help us discover the healing and hope that only Christ can bring. I'm grateful for this book and the difference I know it will make in countless lives.

SISSY GOFF, LPC-MHSP
Bestselling author of *Raising Worry-Free Girls*,
podcast host of the "Raising Boys and Girls" podcast,
and Director of Child and Adolescent Counseling
at Daystar Counseling in Nashville, TN.

BEYOND THE SPIRAL

Why You Shouldn't Believe Everything Anxiety Tells You

**WILL HUTCHERSON &
CHINWÉ WILLIAMS, PH.D.**

Beyond the Spiral: Why You Shouldn't Believe Everything Anxiety Tells You
Published by Orange, a division of The reThink Group, Inc.
5870 Charlotte Lane, Suite 300
Cumming, GA 30040 U.S.A.

Scripture taken from THE MESSAGE. Copyright © 1993, 1994, 1995, 1996, 2000, 2001, 2002. Used by permission of NavPress Publishing Group.

Scripture quotations are taken from the Holy Bible, New Living Translation, Copyright © 1996, 2004, 2015 by Tyndale House Foundation. Used by permission of Tyndale House Publishers, Inc., Carol Stream, Illinois 60188. All rights reserved.

Scripture quotations marked "NIV" are taken from the Holy Bible, New International Version®, NIV®. Copyright © 1973, 1978, 1984, 2011 by Biblica, Inc.™ Used by permission of Zondervan. All rights reserved worldwide. www.Zondervan.com The "NIV" and "New International Version" are trademarks registered in the United States Patent and Trademark Office by Biblica. Inc.™

Get discounted rates on quantities of 10 or more at orangebooks.com.

ISBN: 978-1-63570-206-4
©2023 Will Hutcherson & Chinwé Williams

Writing Team: Will Hutcherson & Chinwé Williams
Lead Editor: Karen Wilson
Creative Direction: Ashley Shugart
Design & Layout: Ashley Shugart & Elizabeth Hildreth
Project Management: Brian Sharp
Director of Publishing: Mike Jeffries
Executive Director of Parent Cue: Hannah Joiner Crosby

Printed in the United States of America
First Edition 2023
1 2 3 4 5 6 7 8 9 10
03/24/23

TABLE
OF CONTENTS

INTRO

We are all afraid of something. Maybe it's heights, speaking in front of large groups, or snakes. The list of fears is endless. Did you know there is even a fear of long words? It's called . . .

Hippopotomonstrosesquippedaliophobia.

Yeah, that's ironic. It's literally one of the longest words in the dictionary, and it's the name for "fear of long words." (By the way, I dare you to try to say that out loud without laughing!)

While feeling fear is a part of life, anxiety doesn't have to keep us from enjoying life. In recent years anxiety has been on the rise. And with that, many voices have emerged on social media channels offering self-help tips to rid you of your anxiety.

While not all these voices and influencers are wrong, there has been a flood of bad advice. Tips and tricks that are not based on sound research. Further, many parents, coaches, teachers, and pastors don't always know how to help.

For those of us who have faith, maybe you've felt like I once did. When I (Will - @willhutch) was in college, I was a new youth pastor facing anxiety. I felt like I had to have it all together, and honestly, I didn't. It wasn't long before I had my first panic attack, and I felt like I was failing in my faith. Maybe I didn't pray enough? Maybe I wasn't trusting God enough?

The reality was I had a need that my brain was trying to communicate. I needed practical tools to move beyond the spiral anxiety was sending me on. Since then, I founded a non-profit called Curate Hope (@curatehope). The Curate Hope team and I speak in schools on mental health. You're probably thinking of boring PowerPoint presentations. Not quite. Our school assemblies are like a dance party with a message of hope.

I (Dr. Chinwé - @dr.chinwewilliams) have been counseling teenagers and adults for nearly twenty years. I started my counseling career as a high school counselor. When I began, I was only a few years older than the oldest senior in the building. So, yes, I felt more than a little anxiety and a pretty good dose of impostor syndrome. I can't think of a single student who didn't struggle with *something at some point*. I supported many of my students through a lot of hard things, such as depression, anxiety, low self-esteem, self-harming, and multiple forms of trauma—you name it, my students experienced it.

My students challenged me in the best possible way, and I remain grateful to God for those years, which have greatly informed my style and approach as a therapist today. I'll never forget what a mentor once told me, "People don't care what you know until they know that you care." We care about you.

In 2021, Will and I wrote *SEEN: Healing Anxiety and Despair in Kids and Teens Through the Power of Connection*. We wrote *SEEN* for anyone wanting to help kids and teenagers with mental health. But as we traveled around the country talking with parents, teens, and college students, we were often asked about what practical tools we could give them to help manage anxiety.

So that's why we wrote this book. To give teens and young adults struggling with anxiety some practical things to do to help them not only cope but thrive.

If you are reading these pages, our guess is that you experience some degree of stress or anxiety. Or, you're concerned about someone you love. Perhaps you have excessive thoughts that seem to be on a constant loop regardless of how many times someone reassures you. Maybe your worries seem more and more difficult to control and leave you feeling keyed up and on edge. Or maybe your stress shows up in your body by way of headaches, stomachaches, and frequent muscle tension. Maybe you just had a panic attack that seemed to come out of nowhere.

Regardless of the situation, we're so happy you grabbed this book.

Research consistently shows that anxiety is the number one mental health problem in America, and maybe even in the world. During the past two decades, panic and anxiety have reached epidemic proportions. Even though anxiety is the most common mental health challenge today, it's also the most treatable.

In this book, we'll talk about the lies we start believing that cause anxiety to spiral and some truths to think about instead. And we'll give you practical action steps, proven to help you take control.

While you don't have to be a Christian to find this book helpful, Will and I have included a section in each chapter for those who are. Our faith plays a huge part in our personal lives and our mental health.

How to Use This Book

There are a few ways you can use this book. You can start in chapter 1 and read page by page. Or you can jump around to the chapters you identify with most. Each chapter stands on its own and has mental health brain boosters. However, we want to encourage you to first read chapter 1, as that will give you context for the "anxiety spiral" that we refer to often throughout the book.

The approach we adopted in this book is holistic, meaning we incorporate strategies that will impact your life on a variety of levels: physically, emotionally, mentally, spiritually, and relationally. Managing your anxiety will often require intervening at different levels. So the chapters in this book will help you identify and express your feelings, understand the role of self-talk, and the importance of lifestyle changes such as nutrition, sleep, and movement. It's easier to counteract the negative effects of anxiety when you're feeling physically healthy and balanced. We even have quizzes, activities, thought exercises, and other relaxation exercises that we think will help make what you are reading really stick.

Many of you reading this book will benefit from sharing what you've learned with a trusted adult, like a parent, mentor, small group leader, or your therapist, if you have one. (If you don't have one, but want one, we share tips on how to find a therapist on page 129). A therapist can help by providing you with some structure and support as you go through some of these concepts and strategies.

Please know that no matter how many times you feel you've messed up or anxiety has gotten the best of you, you won't always feel this way. You don't have to execute these tools perfectly in order for them to work. Each intentional decision you make matters, including the decision to pick up this book.

This book does not and could not possibly address every situation or emotional health challenge you will face. But we will provide you with helpful information that will enable you to better manage anxious feelings.

One last note: Throughout this book, we will tell stories from our experience counseling, guiding, and mentoring teens and young adults. We have changed their names and identifying details for confidentiality. Therefore, any resemblance to actual individuals is merely coincidental.

Thank you for allowing us the privilege of guiding you beyond the spiral of anxiety.

—Will Hutcherson and Dr. Chinwé Williams

BEYOND THE SPIRAL

ONE

MY ANXIETY TOLD ME I WAS DYING

I (Will) was home sick with the flu. For days, I had a low fever, stuffy nose, and a cough. The doctor had given me some medicine earlier in the week. But then Thursday came. I started to feel a sharp pain in my back. Meanwhile, my heart was racing—over 120 beats per minute. I thought, "There must be something wrong with me." So naturally, I Googled it.

I should have known better. Every time I Google something related to health, I usually conclude I'm facing imminent death. Dr. Google told me that I had a 0.001% chance of experiencing an aortic rupture, a fancy way of saying I could die at any moment.

My heart beat even faster.

"See . . . there *is* something wrong with me."

It turns out I wasn't going to die. It was my anxiety trying to convince me I was. After a trip to the hospital and many tests later, they found that the medicine I was taking was causing my heart to race, which in turn caused my back pain. The back pain triggered my fearful thoughts, which in turn caused my heart to race even more.

It cost me a night at the hospital and a lot of money to figure that out. While I'm thankful for the doctors, nurses, and the confirmation that my condition wasn't serious, I have often wondered how it could have turned out if I hadn't believed everything my anxiety told me.

I've always struggled with anxiety though, and chances are that if you're reading this book, you have felt some level of anxiety too. How do we know? Because we have all felt anxiety. According to the National Institute of Mental Health, "Occasional anxiety is a normal part of life."[1]

We all have things we become anxious or worried about in life: a test grade, a job interview, a friend in trouble, a dentist visit. Some levels of anxiety are normal. Anxiety and fear are natural responses to the stressors of life.

In fact, fear can be helpful. Fear is why we don't touch hot stoves or stick our hands in the mouths of bears. It's also why we don't make eye contact with clowns and that scary French teacher with the long fingernails. Fear can help protect us from danger. This is really helpful when we are in real danger, but not so much when we are not in danger. That's when it becomes a problem.

If you are experiencing the kind of anxiety that has taken more control over you than you'd like, you are not alone.

I talk with thousands of teenagers each year in schools about what I've learned about mental health. As a speaker and pastor, I help people navigate mental health challenges with faith in mind. I talk to students on a daily basis who are experiencing anxiety and are desperate to know how to manage it.

As a licensed mental health therapist, Dr. Chinwé has worked with adolescents and young adults for most of her career. Over the years, she has noticed a tremendous rise in the number of her clients struggling with anxiety, which now surpasses depression as the most common mental health challenge in the world.

Not only is anxiety on the rise, but adolescents also have the highest levels of anxiety. The National Institute of Health reported that an estimated one in three adolescents have battled an anxiety disorder, compared to 19% of adults in the same year.[2]

Anxiety isn't just a young person's thing; it's a human thing. However, we know that anxiety looks different and has some unique causes when you're a teenager and young adult. More importantly, we know anxiety can ruin some of the best parts of life during those years.

We've watched thousands of teens and young adults learn to navigate worry, fear, and anxious feelings. We want to give you the same practical and spiritual tools that have helped them. Our hope for you is that as you read through this book, you will discover new ways to take control of your anxiety.

When Does Anxiety Become a Problem?

Since we all have certain levels of anxiety, maybe you're wondering if your anxiety is normal.

Anxiety moves beyond "normal" and becomes a problem when . . .

- Anxiety lasts a long time, affecting your sleep and concentration, or leads to headaches, muscle aches, stomachaches, or unexplained pains.[3]

- You experience panic attacks. These are sudden periods of intense fear, discomfort, or a sense of losing control—even when there is no clear danger or a trigger. This can feel very physical.

- You feel intense fear of being watched or judged by others, making it difficult to be around others. The fear can become so intense that it gets in the way of attending school, working, or hanging out with friends.

- You experience a phobia, a fear that is out of proportion to the real danger. This is usually a fear of an object or a situation. The feeling of worry can be irrational and excessive.

- You feel out of control and unable to manage the feelings of fear or excessive worry.

- You become obsessed with controlling the future or reducing the risk of anything bad happening. Sometimes this can look like obsessive actions or little habits that get in the way of normal actions.

Anxiety Quiz

The questions in this quiz ask about your feelings and thoughts during the last month. In each case, you will be asked to indicate how often you felt or thought a certain way. Although some of the questions are similar, there are differences between them, so treat each one as a separate question. The best approach is to answer fairly quickly. In other words, don't try to count up the number of times you felt a particular way, but give a quick estimate.

....

Next to questions 1-6, write down the number that describes how often you can relate:

0	1	2	3	4
Never	Almost Never	Sometimes	Fairly Often	Very Often

_____ 1. In the last month, how often have you been upset because of something that happened unexpectedly?

_____ 2. In the last month, how often have you felt that you were unable to control the important things in your life?

_____ 3. In the last month, how often have you felt nervous and stressed?

_____ 4. In the last month, how often have you found that you could not cope with all the things you had to do?

_____ 5. In the last month, how often have you been angered because of things that happened that were outside of your control?

_____ 6. In the last month, how often have you felt difficulties were piling up so high that you could not overcome them?

For questions 7-10, use the following scale to describe how often you can relate.

0	1	2	3	4
Very Often	Fairly Often	Sometimes	Almost Never	Never

_____ 7. In the last month, how often have you felt confident about your ability to handle your personal problems?

_____ 8. In the last month, how often have you felt that things were going your way?

_____ 9. In the last month, how often have you been able to control irritations in your life?

_____ 10. In the last month, how often have you felt that you were on top of things?

....

Figuring Your Score

Now add up your scores for each item to get a total.

_____ **My Total Score**

....

Individual scores can range from 0 to 40 with higher scores indicating higher perceived stress, which means you have a higher awareness of stress or anxious feelings.

- Scores **0-13** would be considered **low stress.**

- Scores **14-26** would be considered **moderate stress.**

- Scores ranging from **27-40** would be considered **high perceived stress.**

The Perceived Stress Scale is useful because your perception of what is happening in your life is what is important. Consider the idea that two different people could have the exact same events and experiences in their lives for the past month. Depending on their perception, the total score could put one of those individuals in the low-stress category and put the second person in the high-stress category. In other words, something really stressful for one person may not be as stressful for another.[4]

Continue reading because this book will help you learn specific steps to reduce your stress and anxiety at any level. If, after taking this quiz, you are significantly concerned about your anxiety or overall well-being, please contact your pediatrician or a mental health professional. We provide information on just how to do that in chapter 7.

What Causes Anxiety?

While everyone is different, there are a few situations that will likely contribute to a person's level of anxiety. Becoming aware of what might be causing your anxiety is the first step to overcoming it.

Put a star next to anything on the list below that makes your palms sweat, your stomach knot, your breathing increase, or makes you feel a little extra stressed just thinking about them. Or write down your own.

- **Social events.** Some people experience a level of anxiety while attending parties, hangouts, kickbacks, band trips, or any event with a large group of people. Or feelings of anxiety may arise when feeling excluded from a social event others are attending.

- **Conflict with a friend, family member, or loved one.** No one likes to fight with people who are close to them.

Feeling anxious about the state of a relationship they care about is common when conflict arises.

- **Conflict with strangers.** Maybe a neighbor got mad your dog used their yard to handle their business. Or maybe a friend of a friend said something untrue about you. Or maybe the security guard didn't want you to skateboard on the railing of the stairwell and was a total jerk about it. Regardless the conflict, it could cause anxiety.

- **Too much caffeine.** What you eat and drink can affect your mood, emotional state, and ability to cope with stressors in life. Caffeine tends to be a factor for many in causing feelings of anxiety. (We talk more about this in chapter 4.)

- **Not sleeping enough.** When your brain doesn't have enough downtime, stress can build up in your system. Sleep is a natural process for your brain and body to repair and decompress from the events of the day. (We also talk about this in chapter 4.)

- **Big life changes.** Life changes can be an anxiety starter, especially if the change is unexpected. This can look like the unexpected loss of a loved one or a big move to a new house, city, or school.

- **Personal reminders from stressful past events** (like a sight, sound, smell, or a song that you hear in the grocery store). Sometimes your environment can "take you back," and you are reminded of something from your past that makes you "feel all the feels." This can be a good thing that makes you feel good. We call that nostalgia. But when we are taken back to a moment that was stressful or traumatic, it can feel more like anxiety.

- **Upcoming exams or big presentations.** These take a lot of effort to prepare for and can sometimes leave you feeling a whirlwind of "What ifs" and a fear of failure.[5]

There are a lot of things in our world that can elevate our anxiety. Perhaps you've recognized the turbulence of our world, where national or global news seems to be in constant chaos. My friend Adrian recently shared with me, "I started to feel scared to go to school. I would see videos of school shootings, but I didn't even realize how it affected me." Another friend shared how news of social injustices were increasing her anxiety. One student simply stated how difficult it was to have hope because "Every day, we see something terrible."

The chaos of our world doesn't make navigating anxiety in your life easier. We were never meant to carry so much. But there is hope. Thankfully, feeling peace and strength to overcome anxiety doesn't depend on the stability of the world around us. It's possible to move beyond the spiral of anxiety.

How Anxiety Spirals

When anxiety starts to feel out of control, it can feel like a free-fall spiral. Physically, you may feel a lot of things: racing thoughts, nervousness, panic, increased heart rate, sweating, trembling, fear, trouble concentrating, trouble sleeping, and an upset stomach.

Maybe you can relate to what some teenagers and young adults recently told us:

Anxiety feels like . . .

- ▶ "An elephant sitting on my chest."
- ▶ "Someone else is controlling me."
- ▶ "10,000 thoughts in my head."
- ▶ "Being overpowered."
- ▶ "Lost in thoughts, not knowing how to get out."
- ▶ "Being on edge."
- ▶ "Heart pounding, hands shaking."

Maybe you have experienced anxiety like this, but others have dismissed you, telling you things like . . .

"Just stop overthinking."

"You don't have to feel that way."

"It's just in your head."

"You should just pray more."

Have you ever felt dismissed? Like the way you feel doesn't matter? If so, you may feel not just anxious, but alone. And while you wrestle with all of those very real emotions, maybe you start believing things like . . .

"I'm not safe."

"I just need to ignore it."

"It's all in my head."

"I have no control."

"I don't need help; I can do it alone."

If you've ever felt any of these things, we want you to know that we see you. Anxiety is real, and so are your emotions. But you don't have to get stuck there. **You don't have to believe everything your anxiety is telling you.**

Remember that time when I (Will) thought I was going to die? My anxiety became a problem when I kept circling the worst-case scenario. As I lay on the floor, my anxiety increased, my heart rate increased, and my pain increased. My thoughts caused my heart to race faster, while my heart racing caused more anxious thoughts.

I was stuck in an anxiety spiral, with an irrational fear that I was going to die.

The anxiety spiral is where all the physical senses, feelings, thoughts, and behaviors continue to reinforce each other.

The spiral intensifies until something breaks the spiral. The first loop of the spiral is the normal part of the brain's process. Your first reaction and thought to something stressful is not necessarily full-on anxiety. It could just be a little bit of worry. After the stressor has gone away, or the logical part of your brain has assessed how to cope with the event, your brain breaks out of the spiral. However, when you start believing the lies anxiety tells you, you spiral.

Anxiety has a pattern that starts with an emotion or thought. That thought then creates more emotions and, ultimately, a behavior.

For me, it looked something like this:

- A physical cue from our senses (For me, this was the back pain.)

- A feeling (In my case, I felt FEAR.)

- A thought (My thought: "There is something wrong with me.")

- More physical reactions (Heart racing, increased back pain)

- More feelings (I felt panic.)

- More thoughts ("I must be dying; otherwise, I wouldn't be feeling this way.")

- Behavior (I Googled it.)

The anxiety spiral begins after the second or third loop around. This is when irrational thoughts and lies replace logical thoughts and prevent you from being able to stop the spiral.

Those irrational thoughts are the lies of anxiety. They are like pushing the heart icon on a viral TikTok; they affect the algorithm and just keep the spiral going and going and going.

The Anxiety Spiral

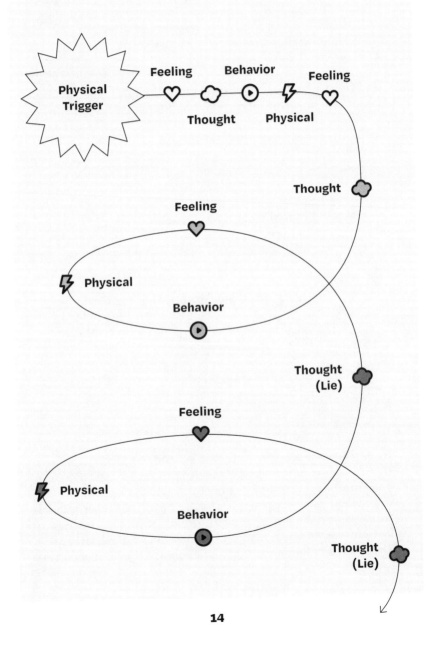

Moving Beyond the Spiral

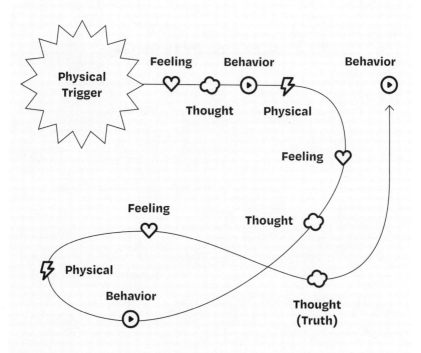

You can move beyond the spiral when you replace the irrational thoughts and the lies of anxiety with a truth. Then, when you reinforce that truth with a behavior, you begin to move back to a baseline of normal thoughts and behaviors, and beyond the spiral of anxiety.

So how do you manage your anxiety? How do you break free from anxiety's grip on your life?

Well, that's what this book is all about—how to get beyond the spiral of anxiety.

Six Lies That Cause Anxiety to Spiral

We have identified six common lies that anxiety tells us.

These lies fuel the anxiety spiral—like adding gas to a fire. These lies also keep someone stuck in anxiety. (Let's clarify something here, though: these aren't always lies. Sometimes you might not be safe in the moment, or you might really miss out on something. The point is, anxiety will eventually turn these thoughts into lies, and that's where the spiral starts.) But when you intentionally replace these lies with truths and actions that reinforce those truths, you can break the spiral and learn to better manage your anxiety.

So here's the good news: You don't have to believe everything anxiety tells you.

Instead, you can interrupt the anxiety spiral and influence your brain to move toward rest and peace by doing these three things:

1. Remind yourself of what's true.

2. Ask yourself, "What can I do?"

3. Ask, "How can I invite God in?"

In each section of this book, we talk about an anxiety lie, replace it with truth, and give you action steps to take with God's help.

The Truth

The "Truth" is the starting point for breaking the anxiety spiral. So this is where we will start in each section. As you focus more on what is true, you can rewire your brain and thought patterns. Our brains are malleable, thanks to neuroplasticity, which means we can change our brains! Over time, you can actually change the structure of your brain through your thinking.[6,7]

What Can I Do?

The "What Can I Do?" section gives you practical steps you can take right away to help you focus more on the truth than the lie anxiety is telling you. These are ground-tested and research-based tools that can help promote mental health and reduce feelings of anxiety. However, it's important to note that these are not instant fixes that you only need to do once. The action steps we share need to be repeated and used with other tools. In other words, if you find a tool helpful, don't stop there. Work on using everything together.

How Can I Invite God In?

If you aren't sure what you think about God or you feel like you are struggling with your faith, don't worry. While we have written this book from a Christian perspective, there are plenty of practical exercises throughout the book that are not spiritual practices. We included this section for people who follow Jesus and struggle with anxiety.

This section in each chapter is where we explore how to invite God into our everyday lives, specifically as we struggle with anxiety. For Dr. Chinwé and me, this is the most important section because God knows a lot about our brains. God made us and knows exactly what we need and has given us brain-boosting spiritual practices to help us. These "ancient pathways" were written in the Bible by numerous authors over the course of thousands of years, and now science and research are showing us how these are really helpful for our mental health. Not only that, they give you a direct line of connection and communication with our Creator, who wants to walk with you every step of the way as you learn to manage your anxiety.

Regardless of how you choose to apply these principles, **the most important thing to know if you are experiencing anxiety is that you won't always feel this way.** There is hope and healing. While you may always struggle with anxiety, you can learn to manage it. Anxiety doesn't have to control your life or keep you from being who you desire to be. You can move beyond the spiral of anxiety.

TWO

THE LIE:
I AM NOT SAFE

"For the longest time, I couldn't figure out why I didn't want to go to school anymore. I just didn't feel like going. It felt weird. Like I would wake up and just start feeling blah. My stomach would hurt a little—like every morning—and I felt tense. After talking with someone I trusted, I realized that I didn't feel safe at school. School shootings were in the news almost every day, and I was just waiting for something to happen at our school. It didn't help that in my junior year, someone called and made a false threat toward our school. We went into a lockdown, and people panicked. No one felt safe that day. But that's how I felt every day."

—Dusty, College Freshman, 19

Have you ever gone through something really, really scary? I mean, like, so scary you wondered if you would even get out alive? I know I have. I (Will) live in Florida. Just about everything in Florida seems dangerous. Florida is wild. It's like everything in Florida wants to eat you or harm you. Even our squirrels seem suspect. We have sharks with sharp teeth. Alligators with sharp teeth. Blood-drinking mosquitoes the size of hummingbirds (that probably have sharp teeth). Florida has hurricanes, tornados, and snakes, and have you ever heard of the "Florida Man?" He's always in the headlines. I mean, it just seems like Florida is a little bit wild. Okay, maybe I'm exaggerating a little. Florida isn't really *that* wild. But we do have some challenges.

Eye of the Hurricane

In 2022, my community was directly hit by an extreme hurricane. The storm was one of the worst hurricanes in Florida's history. In fact, the hurricane that hit my home and my community is now known as the deadliest and most costly hurricane in Florida since 1935. To say this hurricane was a monster is an understatement. Hurricane Ian made other storms in the past seem like rain showers. For more than 12 hours, winds over 155 miles per hour and a major storm surge (which is where water from the ocean comes far up on land) caused catastrophic damage in my community. For more than 12 hours, no one felt safe.

One of my friends, who happens to be one of the toughest guys I know, described the feeling he had when water started rushing into his home. He never imagined a hurricane could bring water to his doorstep since he lives miles from the ocean. He told me experiencing the storm made him feel terrified and fearful for his and his family's lives. Thousands of others in Ian's path felt the same way. After this storm, my friends and I were left picking up the pieces of damaged homes in a broken community. As you can imagine, this created a tremendous amount of stress for all of us, and we experienced waves of grief and loss. Many victims felt their brains were firing with a loud, resounding alarm telling them, "I'm not safe," even after the storm was over.

The Alarm Gets Stuck

For those in the middle of a hurricane, that alarm is accurate. It's not safe to be in the path of a hurricane. But something happened in the weeks and months after Hurricane Ian. Many people in my community were still experiencing the alarm, "I'm not safe," in their minds. For some, it was like the alarm was stuck. And my friend Matt, even a month after the storm, still felt shaken up.

One of the foundational and convincing lies anxiety tells us is "I'm not safe." The reality is this is a half-truth. Because when we receive this message from our brains originally, it's probably true. At some point, you probably didn't feel safe. Like in my friend's case, he really wasn't safe in the middle of a hurricane. But afterward, when he was physically safe, he didn't *feel* safe right away. That's because when our brains go into emergency mode, they release a ton of survival hormones.

Hormones like cortisol and adrenaline are really helpful when we are in immediate danger. These hormones increase our awareness so we can navigate dangerous situations. But there are times when so many of these chemicals are released in our bodies that it causes us to stay on edge. **Our brains can get stuck with this tiny little message deep inside the amygdala** (more on that shortly)**, screaming like a repeating alarm, "I'm not safe."**

It's not only the big storms in life that make us feel unsafe. Sometimes it's small things. Like new situations. Starting a new job or starting at a new school. Or feeling uncertain about the future. Big or small, some things can make us feel like we're not safe relationally, physically, or emotionally.

Think of it like this: **Anxiety can be like a leaky faucet.** A little drip over time produces a lot of water. In the same way, when you are experiencing stress after stress, cortisol (your body's main stress hormone) can get stuck like a leaky faucet. It just keeps dripping. This drip usually comes from the brain perceiving a lack of safety, even from small things. After a while, you may even start to think, "I'm always going to feel this way."

Once you are out of a scary situation, you *should* feel safe again. **But anxiety takes the past and projects it into the future.** For instance, if I experience a car crash that makes me feel afraid, that feeling is true in real time, but it may cause me not to feel safe the next time I'm in a car. This is an example of taking a past circumstance and projecting it into the future with worry and fear.

This type of anxiety is caused by traumatic stress. The American Psychological Association (APA) defines trauma as "an emotional response to a terrible event."[8] This happens when you feel emotionally hurt or alarmed by an event. Examples of traumatic events include a vehicle crash, a difficult breakup or loss of a relationship, the death of a loved one, or a natural disaster like a tornado, hurricane, or earthquake.

Following a traumatic or terrifying event, it makes sense to have an emotional reaction that continues even when you are not in danger anymore.

Fear is a natural human emotion and one that everyone experiences. Whatever caused you to feel unsafe initially was real, and those lingering thoughts and that steady drip of anxiety you might be experiencing is completely understandable. What matters most is how you fight your fears. We want to teach you what we believe are helpful strategies to support you as you do.

THE TRUTH: I WON'T ALWAYS FEEL THIS WAY

While it may feel like you are stuck in a cycle of anxiety, there is hope. Because you won't always feel this way. Your brain is wired to respond to stress in a way that helps you feel safe. But it is also reprogrammable, even when it starts to go a little haywire. So, how do you reprogram the brain and break free from the cycle of anxiety? First, you need to understand what is actually happening in your brain. So geek out with us for a minute; this is actually quite fascinating.

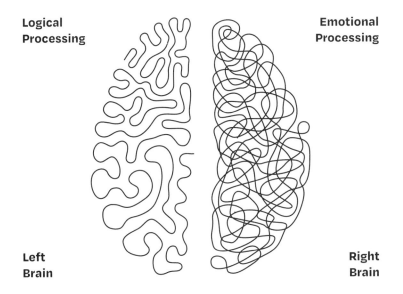

**Logical
Processing**

**Emotional
Processing**

**Left
Brain**

**Right
Brain**

How Your Brain Works

Your brain responds to stress in predictable ways. Research shows us that a series of processes happen when we experience stress. Let us explain.

The brain is made up of two parts. Actually, it's made up of a lot of parts. But we're going to break it down into two halves and two essential functions.[9]

The *right* side of the brain is responsible for emotional processing. This is where the amygdala (a tiny little almond-sized part of your brain) processes fear and other emotions that activate the "fight, flight, or freeze" response during stressful or dangerous situations. Depending on the circumstance and how you are wired, you may react to danger in different ways. You will either face it and confront the danger, run away from it or avoid it, or freeze up and not be able to react at all.

I like to think of the amygdala, where all this commotion is happening, as a little tiny uptight almond person named Amy. If the brain were a community, Amy would be super serious, always looking for something suspicious. Like the nosy neighbor peering out their window.

The *left* side of the brain is responsible for logical processing. This is the part of the brain where one's ability to plan and organize takes place. When you're calm, the left brain is able to be logical. But when you're upset, the right brain can take over and react from an emotional place. That's when overly-protective and unpredictable Amy takes charge. This happens even more with anyone who has had a previous traumatic experience.

In a healthy brain, processing goes back and forth between the two sides—emotional and logical. God designed your brain so you can feel many different emotions, but you're able to flip your brain over to cognitive processing. In other words, your emotions are *real*, but you have the ability to consider them logically and determine whether what you feel is actually *true*.

For example, if I hear a loud bang followed by the sound of shattering glass, I will instinctively be startled. Let's look at the spiral again using this example.

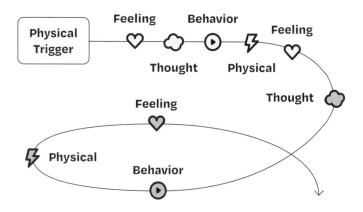

- **Physical sensation =** I hear glass shattering.

- **Feeling =** I feel fear.

- **Thought =** A bear must have broken into my house. (Okay, maybe not a bear. After all, bears don't break into houses. It's probably a rabid squirrel.)

- **Behavior =** Fight, Flight, or Freeze. My heart rate will rise, as I would likely go into fight mode, grabbing the closest thing next to me, ready to attack—even if the closest item happens to be a couch pillow. Or I may just get up and run away as fast as I can and crawl under the bed. Depending on the day, I might not be able to react at all and just freeze and not move a muscle. I'd likely hold my breath and tense up every muscle.

But I can disrupt this cycle. Let's say after I hear the crash, I stop and look around. This engages the left side of my brain. By looking around, I am investigating (logical processing), and I discover that a picture has fallen off the wall. I logically conclude that the picture must have made the noise and that an armed, crazy-eyed llama didn't break into my house. (Don't get me started on the untrustworthiness of llamas. I've seen things.) Once I've logically processed that I'm not in danger, I take a deep breath, and my stress begins to subside.

Healthy functioning means we're able to deal with our emotions properly. The problem is, when we can't logically process our emotions, something else takes place: **anxiety.** And unchecked anxiety can lead to **despair,** a place where we never really feel safe at all.

When my friend Malike and I go to schools and speak to students, we often explain it this way: "Anxiety is an obsession with the future, and depression is an obsession with the past. So what do we miss? The present."

So what can we do to battle the lie "I'm not safe?" Focus on being present . . . right here . . . this moment . . . today.

WHAT CAN I DO? JUST BREATHE

Do me a favor. Right now. Notice your breath. Are you breathing normally? Deeply? Shallow? Are you holding your breath?

Did you know there is a connection between your emotional state and your breath? When we are feeling fearful, we tend to hold our breath. When we are feeling anxious, we take short, shallow breaths. When we are relaxed or joyful, our breathing is slow and more rhythmic. This all happens unconsciously.

Breathing *as if* you're relaxed helps the body regulate the fight-or-flight response that happens when you're worried or stressed out. Slowing the pace of your breathing is especially helpful if you're restless and anxious about what happened earlier today—or what might happen tomorrow or next week.

One of the best and simplest ways to quiet the anxious mind is to focus on your breathing and engage in slow, deep breaths. Deep breathing is very therapeutic because it lowers your heart rate, helps you think more rationally, and can calm your emotions. Taking slow and deep breaths is called conscious breathing, and it's been proven very effective in managing anxiety. It's pretty easy to learn.

How Should I Breathe?

If you're like me, when someone says, "Focus on your breathing," you immediately start overthinking it and somehow forget how to breathe. But don't worry; we'll walk you through it. Here is a breathing exercise you can practice whenever you want to feel less anxious or just more relaxed and aware.

4-7-8 Breathing Technique

One of my favorite breathing techniques to relax the mind and body is called 4-7-8, also known as "conscious breathing." It is super simple, takes almost no time, and can be done anywhere.

While learning this exercise, keep your back straight. Place the tip of your tongue just behind your upper front teeth, and keep it there throughout the entire exercise.

1. Purse your lips as if you are about to blow out a candle.

2. Exhale completely through your mouth, making a whoosh sound.

3. Close your mouth and inhale quietly through your nose to a mental count of **four.**

4. Hold your breath for a count of **seven.**

5. Exhale completely through your mouth, making a whoosh sound to a count of **eight.** This is one breath.

6. Now inhale again and repeat the cycle three more times for a total of four breaths.

7. *Note:* Always inhale quietly through your nose and exhale audibly through your mouth. The tip of your tongue stays in position the whole time.

8. Exhalation takes twice as long as inhalation.

9. The total amount of time spent on each phase of breathing doesn't matter; the ratio 4:7:8 is what's important.

Inhale
(4 Seconds)

Hold
(7 Seconds)

Exhale
(8 Seconds)

For more support, you can practice breathing alongside Dr. Chinwé as she demonstrates a few techniques:

Calm is a popular App that can help you practice breathing. It's free but has premium features.

HOW CAN I INVITE GOD IN? KNOW GOD IS ALWAYS WITH ME

Christians can sometimes give advice about anxiety that isn't exactly helpful, saying things like, "If you would just trust God more, then you wouldn't be struggling with anxiety. If you prayed more, you would experience peace." But we know that's easier said than done. Those well-meaning phrases often throw us back into despair because they don't always feel very helpful when we are trapped in the anxiety spiral.

As a therapist, Dr. Chinwé trains her clients in various coping skills (like conscious breathing) that are proven very effective at managing anxiety and stress. We will talk about many of those skills throughout the book. Combined with these strategies, the best hope we have in navigating our mental health is to look to our Creator, our ultimate hope, the One who knows every struggle we face, every thought, and every worry.

The coping strategies we give you in this book work because of the way God created our bodies and our minds to function.

For instance, God gave you the ability to control your breathing and be deliberate in getting essential oxygen when you need it to calm your stress. So when you use practices like this while at the same time inviting God, your Creator, to walk with you through your anxiety, you have a powerful strategy to help you stand against all of anxiety's clever lies.

There is a lot about anxiety and fear in the Bible, by the way, and what to do when we don't feel safe. We found 167 occurrences in the Bible where we are told to **"not be afraid."**[10] God obviously knew we would struggle with that one on a daily basis. Usually, when God tells His people not to be afraid, it is for that particular moment and reminds them that He is with them. It's important to note that God is not saying to never be afraid in your whole life because feeling fear is part of being human.

But how can we feel safe when we don't feel safe? God wants you to know you aren't alone through it all. God will walk with you every step of the way, guiding you and helping you conquer your anxious thoughts.

> "So do not fear, for I am with you;
> do not be dismayed, for I am your God.
> I will strengthen you and help you;
> I will uphold you with my righteous right hand"
> (Isaiah 41:10, NIV).

The greatest example of God being with us is Jesus. God left heaven to come and walk among us. Jesus is the example of "God with us." Years ago, Jesus came, walked this earth, and experienced human life, with human emotions and human needs. Jesus ate food like we do and felt emotions like we do. But He also did things that only God can do. Jesus allowed Himself to die as a sacrifice for our sin and mistakes. And then three days later, He rose from the grave, overcoming the greatest human challenge, death itself. Jesus asks us to trust Him, not just for our eternity, but in our human experience on earth as well.

So take a deep breath, and remember that God is with you. He's always been there. So invite God into your story, into your struggle, and into your anxious thoughts. **Let God walk with you on this journey, knowing you can feel safe because God is ALWAYS with you.**

On a scale of 1 to 10, how anxious do you feel right now?

_____

What helps you feel safe?

_____

_____

_____

How can you invite God into your anxiety? (We'll show you a few ways throughout this book.)

_____

_____

_____

In what ways have you seen God show up in your past fears, worries, and thoughts?

_____

_____

_____

Recap

The foundational lie that anxiety tells you is that you are not safe—which triggers your fight, flight, or freeze mechanism in your brain and causes your anxiety to spiral. While there may be times when you don't feel safe, the reality is that sometimes we get stuck in our fear. So remember that you will be okay and that you won't always feel this way. The best thing to do in these moments is to just breathe and remember that no matter what happens, you don't have to be afraid because God is always with you.

THE LIE
I am not safe.

THE TRUTH
I won't always feel this way.

WHAT CAN I DO?
Just breathe.

HOW CAN I INVITE GOD IN?
Know God is always with me.

THREE

THE LIE:
I SHOULD JUST IGNORE IT

"My biggest problem is being okay with sharing my emotions. I didn't realize it at first, but when I started to see a counselor when I was 15, I realized I was stuffing all my anxiety and feelings. Stuffing my emotions was a big source of the panic attacks I would have. I felt insecure at times. When my friends forgot to invite me somewhere, I felt excluded. When my sister gave her friend the homecoming dress she already told me I could borrow, I felt betrayed and angry. But I never told anyone. I just said, 'It's okay, no big deal.' But on the inside, it was a big deal, I just figured my emotions didn't matter, and I just needed to get over it.

My counselor told me I had an anger management problem and that I needed to allow myself to get angry and let people know when I felt let down and upset. I had to learn that my emotions matter and that ignoring them doesn't help. So, I started to carry a journal and write down what I was feeling. I practiced being more honest with others about how I was feeling. It helped A LOT! Now I still feel anxious at times, but I am doing better at sharing how I feel instead of just ignoring it."

—Kayla, High School Junior, 17

Maybe you can relate to Kayla's story. You hear your anxiety tell you things like . . .

"My emotions don't matter."

"I just need to get over it."

"I need to suck it up."

"I'm just not an emotional person."

"It's no big deal."

All of these are rooted in the lie "I should just ignore it."

After all, maybe we tend to think that if we ignore our anxiety, it will just go away. But ignoring something is rarely the solution. This is especially true with anxiety. It might feel like ignoring anxiety works for a short time, but when we ignore our emotions, we tend to stuff them—meaning your emotions are still there. You're just hiding them down inside somewhere. So they don't go away; they actually show up bigger later. And the consequences may be more serious than you might think. A study by the Harvard School of Public Health and the University of Rochester showed that people who bottled up their emotions increased their chance of premature death by more than 30 percent and their risk of being diagnosed with cancer by 70 percent.[11]

When you ignore your anxiety, you're just deferring for a later spiral date. It takes you further down the anxiety spiral path, so the next time you feel stressed or anxious, you are building on where we left off.

Think of it like a lake with a dam. One anxious event adds more water to the lake. Without an outlet, the water continues to fill up until it can't hold any more. Eventually, the water spills over or the pressure on the dam becomes so high that the dam breaks and water escapes at a rapid rate. Or think of it like that notification that sent you over the edge. You know that random app on your phone that just feels the need to notify you *constantly*?

Most of the time you just swipe them away and ignore them, but then it eventually hits that point where you just can't handle it anymore so you delete the app or throw your phone into the lake with the dam.

THE TRUTH: MY EMOTIONS MATTER

The anxiety spiral that is fueled by the lie "I should just ignore it" leads to stuffing. And stuffing leads to one of two destinations:

You will either implode or explode.

In other words, you could be a volcano or a sinkhole.

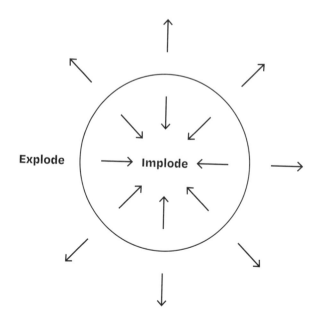

Depending on how you're wired, you might be prone to be either an imploder or an exploder when it comes to releasing the strong emotions you feel. Our friend Sissy Goff talks about these sometimes unhelpful coping skills in her book, *Raising Worry-Free Girls.*[12] Let me explain it this way. Have you ever tried to hold your breath for as long as you could? Imagine you breathe in a big breath of air—the biggest breath ever. But now imagine that you hold it in for as long as possible. While your lungs are completely filled, you tighten up your lips not to let even a wisp of air out of your body. After a few moments, your face turns red. You might even begin to shake as you tighten up your body to hold in this big breath. Eventually, after a few seconds or minutes, what happens? One of two events will take place. You will either:

- Exhale with an eruption of air all at once, or

- You will pass out and start breathing again. (By the way, don't try that.)

The same happens with your emotions. When you ignore your emotions and just keep stuffing or dismissing them, it's like when you have this big breath of emotion that you are trying to hold in. When you ignore your emotions, you leave tons of emotional energy in the brain. To deal with that excess energy, the brain triggers a defense mechanism called emotional detachment. This is like an emotional numbing, where you don't feel strongly about anything. This can be temporary or long-lasting. Internalizing our emotions in this way can eventually lead us to either emotionally implode or explode.

Here's the point: **Emotions come out eventually.**

What Do Emotional Implosions Look Like?

Emotional imploding is like a sinkhole. A sinkhole happens over time in places like Florida, where I (Will) live. This is when moving water under the surface of the ground wears out the ground, causing it to collapse. The water under the surface is unseen, and the weight on the surface is heavy. Emotional imploding happens in a similar way. **The unseen stuffed emotions wear down your resilience and your ability to handle stress and the weight of the world. Over time, you start to fall apart.**

Emotional imploding can happen when you stuff emotions. This looks like an internal swirling that can leave you feeling on edge. Have you ever been in a conflict with someone and you walk away thinking about all the things you wished you had said—for the next few hours? Your emotions and feelings start to swirl. Eventually, you may journal about it, talk with a friend, or try to resolve the conflict with the person. But what if you didn't? You would stuff the feelings and hope they go away. And what happens when you see that person again? Usually, if you had strong emotions that were unresolved, regardless of how much time has passed, you would feel the swirling again.

The problem with stuffing emotions is that, eventually, they *will* surface in one way or another. You implode with emotional energy that releases through panic attacks, obsessive actions, or feelings of despair.

If you are prone to stuff emotions and implode like a sinkhole, you may have thought something like, "Where did that come from?" You'd be right to ask that because there is usually a deeper source for your outbursts.

Emotional implosions can look like any of the following:

Panic Attacks

Panic attacks are very physical. The physical response from our bodies makes panic attacks feel like much more than just a mild worry. They are a full-blown implosion. Here are a few symptoms:

- ▸ Sense of impending doom or danger
- ▸ Fear of loss of control or death
- ▸ Rapid, pounding heart rate
- ▸ Sweating
- ▸ Trembling or shaking

- Shortness of breath or tightness in your throat
- Chills
- Hot flashes
- Nausea
- Abdominal cramping
- Chest pain
- Headache
- Dizziness, lightheadedness, or faintness
- Numbness or tingling sensation
- Feeling of unreality or detachment[13]

Although panic attacks can happen anytime, many people experience them at night as they start to settle from the day. Once, I was reading a book that happened to tell the story of someone experiencing a loss. This was a trigger for me. Simply reading an intense story sent me into an anxiety spiral, and before I knew it, I was having a panic attack. **(See page 51 on how to manage a panic attack.)**

Obsessive Behaviors

Obsessive behaviors are another example of how we implode our emotions. The clinical term you've likely heard before is called OCD or obsessive-compulsive disorder. Those who have an OCD diagnosis or OCD tendencies feel compelled to do repeated behaviors (compulsions) due to unwanted thoughts and fears (obsessions) in order to feel calmer. It is not uncommon for someone struggling with anxiety to have fears or thoughts that lead to compulsions.

Unfortunately, in our culture, the term OCD is often misrepresented and used to label people who are particular about something. But OCD is more than just being particular or having a preference. OCD is a disorder that interferes with one's daily life and is usually undesired. The truth is that those experiencing OCD really want to stop and do not want to keep experiencing those unwanted, repetitive thoughts or fears. Often, this is a result of below-the-surface feelings or thoughts that lead to these behaviors. The brain reacts this way to attempt to soothe anxious thoughts or feelings. However, the relief is usually short-lived and can sometimes affect normal functioning.

Depression

The last example of emotional implosion is depression. This is the biggest danger to stuffing our emotions. Depression is a mood disorder that can range from mild to severe and from temporary (or situational) to prolonged. Let's look at a few of these differences.

Situational depression is a temporary condition that occurs when an individual has difficulty coping with or adjusting to a major life change, crisis, or event. Situational depression develops as a reaction to an extremely stressful event. Although situational depression can sometimes feel almost as heavy and dismal as clinical depression, it doesn't typically involve as many of the more severe symptoms, such as suicidal thoughts, and it goes away once the stressful situation has resolved.

Clinical depression. If someone you care about is clinically depressed, what they are experiencing goes well beyond teenage "moodiness." Clinical depression, also known as major depression, is a severe form of depression where feelings of sadness and inadequacy are persistent.[14]

Symptoms of clinical depression include:

- Continued sadness and hopelessness
- Feelings of guilt or worthlessness
- Pervasive worry and anxiety
- Loss of interest in once enjoyable activities
- Lack of energy and fatigue
- Withdrawal from friends or loved ones, or isolation
- Lack of concentration, difficulty with memory, or difficulty making decisions
- Sleeping too little or sleeping too much
- Unexplained aches and pains
- Thoughts of self-harm
- Preoccupation with death or thoughts of dying

Different from despair, someone struggling with clinical depression experiences most of these symptoms most of the day, nearly every day, and it impacts their overall functioning. It is worth mentioning that in order to be diagnosed with clinical depression by a mental health professional, an individual would have to exhibit several of these symptoms for at least two weeks. It is important not to self-diagnose but rather talk to a mental health professional or doctor if you think you are experiencing clinical depression.

Despair

One of my best friends struggles with anxiety and clinical depression. There have been moments in his life where despair has crept in. Moments when it's been hard for him to even get off the floor. It's hard to watch someone you care about feel so hopeless. Maybe you've had moments like that.

Despair, like depression, can be temporarily debilitating. Despair is a profound feeling of discouragement and negativism about most things, particularly the future.

Many teens and young adults facing despair often express feelings of . . .

- ▸ pain
- ▸ anguish
- ▸ loss of hope
- ▸ loss of joy

However, despair differs from episodes of clinical depression in that people can typically (but not always) complete daily tasks. For example, they may be able to attend school, athletic events, or small group meetings and function somewhat normally despite their overwhelming feelings of heaviness.[15]

Whether it's despair or depression, the pain or anguish may become so intense that some people think about taking their lives.

The feeling of hopelessness can intensify to the point that you (or someone you know) can even feel like you're caught in a trap:

1. You can't imagine the pain ever stopping.

2. You can't imagine ever feeling happy again.

3. You can't imagine living a life that makes a difference in the world.

The inner dialogue might sound like this: "All I need to do is kill myself, and my problems and pain will be over, and I won't be a burden to other people." If that terrible thought makes sense to you or someone you know, it means you (or they) have probably lost joy, hope, and value. In moments like these, your problems feel like they will last forever. So giving up on life now might seem like an option that makes sense.

But hear me out. This is really important.

Don't make a permanent decision because of a temporary problem or feeling.

You won't always feel the way you feel. There is always hope. Think of it this way: When we can't see the truth, lies begin to make sense instead. We start to follow the lies and do what they say. We let them LEAD us.

And that's a problem because . . . well, they're lies.

When we believe them and act on them, we can end up missing out on the good things in life. The lie that I need to hurt myself or give up on the gift of life is the most dangerous lie there is. If you (or someone you know) are experiencing thoughts of hurting yourself or ending your life, please talk with someone. You matter. Your feelings matter. Talk to a trusted adult if you are experiencing these thoughts in any form.

If you aren't sure who to talk to or need immediate help, call or text the National Crisis Helpline at 988 (in the United States).

What Do Emotional Explosions Look Like?

Similar to emotionally imploding, emotional exploding can happen when you stuff or dismiss your emotions until you finally explode. We all know people who have emotionally exploded like a volcano.

Emotional explosions look like fits of rage, outbursts of anger, or a variety of emotions all at once.

Anger, Bitterness, and Rage

Remember, it's okay to be angry. Let me say that again for the people in the back: **It is okay to be angry.**

Anger is an emotion; it's just a feeling. You might need to be angry. To just let it go. No, really, it's okay. In fact, it's necessary. Anger has a bad rap in our culture. Many people are shamed for their anger, and over time culture teaches us that we should repress it. You've probably heard the phrase, "Holding onto anger is like drinking poison and expecting the other person to die."

Holding on to anger is different from simply feeling angry. The problem, as you already know by this point, is that our emotions will come out eventually. This is true for anger as well. The question is, how will it come out? If we hold on to anger, it becomes poison. But if we allow ourselves to process and feel anger in healthy ways (more on that later), anger can be a fuel for positive behavior.

Anger is an emotion, not an action. So just because we feel angry doesn't mean we must act aggressively. In fact, anger is usually paired with other emotions. We often label our emotions as "angry" when we really feel unsafe, misunderstood, or scared. Further, we can feel anger when something breaks our hearts. I know the sadness and anger I feel when I see injustice in the world.

When I see poor people being taken advantage of or children being mistreated, it's heartbreaking. And it makes me angry. That anger is a fuel that I use to work toward positive change when I have the opportunity.

The racial injustice in America made Martin Luther King Jr. passionately angry. You can hear the heartbreak and anger in his words and tone when you listen to his speeches. But MLK didn't use that anger as fuel for hatred, bitterness, or violence. He used it for positive change. This is another example of the positive side of anger.

However, anger can turn into something more dangerous, like bitterness, hatred, and rage. Bitterness and hatred that swirl around in one's mind can cause more harm than you would think. Studies have shown that suppressed anger (bitterness) causes trouble in your relationships and can also cause disease. (We will talk more about how the body and mind are connected in chapter 5). Bitterness and hatred can eventually result in the kind of explosion that causes maximum damage: Rage.

The Merriam-Webster dictionary defines rage as "a violent and uncontrolled anger."[16] Rage is a destructive force and behavior that is often expressed in violence. So while it's okay to feel anger, it's important to understand the dangers of suppressing anger that can turn into bitterness, hatred, or rage.

Again, here's the main idea: **Emotions come out eventually.**

You can stuff and dismiss your emotions and wait for an implosion or an explosion, or you can take healthy steps to acknowledge your emotions on a regular basis.

Your emotions matter.

Over time, we can start to believe the lie that our emotions don't matter. Maybe you've had others tell you things like:

"Stop crying."

"You don't need to worry about that."

"That's silly to feel that way; it doesn't make sense."

"Just get over it."

But your emotions do matter. It's just a question of what to do with them.

WHAT CAN I DO? FEEL EMOTIONS

Every emotion is valid, and every emotion is real. But here's the thing: Just because it's valid doesn't mean your belief that caused the emotion is true. And it doesn't mean you should always act on how you feel. Because acting on your feelings can leave you with regrets. However, every feeling is important enough to be acknowledged.

An emotion is just an emotion. That's it. So, you should acknowledge emotions for what they are.

Let's say I accidentally walk into the wrong classroom while the teacher is teaching. Immediately, I realize my mistake, but now everyone is looking at me, and the teacher stops teaching. With everyone looking at me, my face turns red because I feel embarrassed. I say, "Oops, wrong class," but my voice cracks as I do. The situation just got even worse! Now, I feel humiliated when I hear a few laughs from other students as I walk out the door. For the rest of the day, I keep replaying that three-second moment in my head, my thoughts and emotions swirling.

At this point, I have a choice. I can ignore those feelings, or I can acknowledge them. Writing about the experience later or talking with a friend can be helpful, but the important part is for me to identify the emotions and process them for a few moments. I need to resist the urge to allow my processing to reinforce a negative lie like, "I'm so stupid" or "I should have known better." Both options lead to shame.

How Can Processing Emotions Help?

Acknowledging emotions interrupts the spiral. Just like you can't get a boiling pot of water to stop boiling by placing a lid on it, you can't get excessively worrisome thoughts to simply stop by ignoring or avoiding them. You have to turn down the temperature on the stove if you want the water to simmer down, and the same is true for a mind heating up with worries. You have to turn down the emotional temperature to cool off. How do you do that? Begin by bringing calm, cool awareness to your emotions.

Remember the example of taking in a big breath of air? You can only hold your breath until you either explode or you pass out. So instead of letting your emotions out all at once or becoming numb to your emotions, you can pause and exhale your emotions. You can do this by being deliberate in taking time to acknowledge big feelings and spending some time with them. This processing allows you to move your emotions from one side of the brain to the logical side of your brain. Once you make the switch, you can then draw conclusions and make better decisions. And you won't be acting on pure emotion.

How Do I Emotionally Exhale?

You can practice exhaling emotionally in a few different ways:

1. **Identify the emotion.**
    To exhale an emotion, you must first name it. A tool that we like to use is a Feelings Wheel. Most of us do not have a large emotional vocabulary, so a feelings wheel like the one on page 48 can be helpful.[16] Start in the middle with the easily identifiable emotions. These are core emotions. From there, you can look at the secondary emotions, working yourself toward the outer rim. Once you find that emotion, acknowledge it.

2. **Feel the emotion.**

When you acknowledge emotions, you don't need to draw conclusions; just allow yourself to feel the emotion. Remember, feelings are just feelings. To feel the emotion, you have to accept it for what it is. Just an emotion. Resist the urge to feel guilty or ashamed. Don't go down the thought pattern "Well, I shouldn't feel this way" or "I should feel another way." Just take it for what it is, then act. Most importantly, don't ignore it.

3. **Exhale the emotion.**

To exhale the emotion, you need to move it to the logical side of your brain. The key to exhaling the emotion is communication. But that's not the only way. You can go for a run, scream into your pillow, or find another healthy way to express strong emotions. Some people find art to be a helpful outlet. If you have a friend or family member nearby, you can share with them. But only share with people who won't dismiss your emotion or shame your emotion.

Journaling can be helpful here as well. (We will talk more about how to do this in chapter 5.)

You can ask yourself:

- ▸ How did I feel?
- ▸ What did I conclude or believe?
- ▸ Is what I believed true, helpful, or kind?
- ▸ What action did I take?
- ▸ What can I do in the future?

How Do I Handle Anger?

Our culture has a way of handling some emotions in extremes. On one side, culture might tell you emotions like anger are bad and must be avoided. On the other hand, if I feel angry, everyone on TikTok is going to know and needs to know about it. So let's take a look at how you might deal with anger when your blood starts to boil.

Eugene Peterson, the author of *The Message Bible,* translated Paul's (one of Jesus' early followers) words this way:

> "Go ahead and be angry. You do well to be angry—but don't use your anger as fuel for revenge. And don't stay angry. Don't go to bed angry. Don't give the Devil that kind of foothold in your life" (Ephesians 4:26-27, MSG).

You do well to be angry. Let it out. Be angry . . . at least for a little while.

The point is, it doesn't help to stuff your anger. Instead, manage anger in a healthy and helpful way. Let it out so it doesn't fester into bitterness and internal rage. Or let it out before it comes out later in snarky, passive-aggressive comments.

How to process anger:

1. Accept that you feel angry.

2. Feel the emotion fully.

3. Communicate it. Write your emotions down or talk to someone you trust.

4. Get the energy out. Anger can produce a surge of cortisol or adrenaline. Find a way to express your anger in a healthy way. Go for a run or walk, punch your pillow, buy a punching bag, or rip up some paper. The idea is to express your anger in healthy ways, not in ways that hurt you or others.

Feelings Wheel

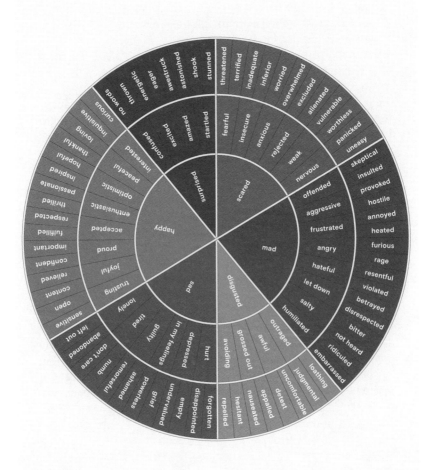

Name Your Feelings Exercise

1. Use the feelings wheel on the opposite page to practice naming your feelings. Start in the inner circle with the six easily identifiable emotions.

2. Ask yourself, "What is the secondary emotion I'm feeling?" It's possible to feel more than one.

3. Take some time to process, journal, or talk with someone about your feelings.

Coping with Panic Attacks

Panic attacks are familiar to me (Dr. Chinwé), not just professionally, but also personally. My mom was going over the West Ashley bridge in Charleston, South Carolina, when she had her first panic attack. She was so frightened that she stopped the car. Right there. Yes, right over one of the largest and scariest bridges in the Holy City (the name given to Charleston due to the number of churches clustered together). Until this day, I still feel a slight wave of fear in the pit of my stomach when I think about how petrified my mom must've been. I remember she kept repeating that it seemed like the panic symptoms just came "out of nowhere."

If you've ever experienced a panic attack, you know that it is one of the most intensely uncomfortable and downright scary feelings a human can experience. A panic attack is a sudden episode of intense fear that often seems to have no apparent cause. That's why many people say that the attack seemingly occurred "out of the blue."

Panic attacks **feel** *very* physical because they are. Common bodily symptoms include shortness of breath, dizziness, sweating, tingling in the hands and feet, and tightening in the chest (hence that heart-attack feeling).

When a panic attack hits, you are convinced that you're losing control, having a heart attack, or even dying.

As a therapist, I've worked with many clients who have had full-fledged panic attacks, leaving them feeling terrified and helpless, wondering when the next one will hit.

Over the years, I have counseled clients who experience panic attacks in the car, on the lacrosse field, or while on a mission trip. Yes, they can happen almost anywhere, but the one thing they tend to have in common is that other factors are typically building up, eventually leading to the attack.

Although it **feels** like it, panic attacks rarely **appear** out of the blue.

One of my clients, let's call her Chrissy, was 19 when she experienced a really sad break-up, which she initially thought she was handling well. She didn't talk to anyone about how she was feeling, but again, she thought she was doing pretty okay. But after a week of restless and tearful nights tossing and turning while ruminating on every aspect of the relationship and what she could have missed, something had to give. She experienced her first panic attack, ten days after the breakup, around 4:00 a.m.

Panic creeps up when you're sleep-deprived and over-tired. (Another reason to prioritize sleep. We'll talk about that more soon.) Although panic attacks are rarely life-threatening, they can be intensely frightening.

If you battle with occasional or frequent panic attacks, the *good* news is you can learn to manage and even diminish panic attacks.

There are some tips on the next two pages that will help.

How Do I Manage a Panic Attack?

1. **Remind yourself that it will pass.**

   - While very frightening in the moment, panic attacks typically reach their most intense point within ten minutes of their onset, then begin to subside.

   - Try to remind yourself that this is a brief period of intense anxiety and will be over soon.

   - No one has ever been seriously harmed from a panic attack.

2. **Slow down your breath.**

   - Panic attacks can cause shallow and rapid breathing and make feelings of anxiety and body tension worse.

   - Slowing down and deepening your breath can help bring a panic attack under control and begin to relax your body and your mind.

   - Practice the 4-7-8 breathing protocol. (see page 27) Breathe deeply in from your abdomen for four seconds, hold the breath for seven seconds, then exhale slowly for eight seconds. Repeat three times.

3. **Focus on a specific object.**

   - When overwhelming or upsetting thoughts, feelings, or memories surface, focusing on something concrete in the environment can help you feel more grounded.

   - Grounding techniques can help reduce the symptoms of a panic attack. Here are some you can try:

     ▸ Focus on a photo, painting, or mark on the wall. As you concentrate on it, think about what it looks like, how it feels, who created it, its shape, and texture.

> ▸ If you experience frequent panic attacks, try
> carrying a familiar object to help ground you (a
> smooth stone, a cross, a seashell, a stress ball, or
> a smooth vial of lavender essential oil to sniff).

4. Try the 5-4-3-2-1 method.

Panic attacks aren't only scary; they can make you feel detached from reality. That's because the intensity of the anxious thoughts and sensations can hijack your other senses. This method is a grounding technique that helps direct your focus away from internal feelings of overwhelm. Here's how it works. Try not to rush. Be sure to complete each step thoughtfully:

- **Look at 5 separate objects.** Look around for five things you can see, and say them out loud. For example, you could say, "I see my phone, I see the computer, I see the water bottle, I see the picture frame, I see my pen." Think about each one for a few seconds.

- **Touch 4 things around you.** Start with your body and think of four things you can feel, and say them out loud. For example, you could say, "I feel my feet warm in my socks," or "I feel the seat that I am sitting on." Consider their texture, temperature, and their uses.

- **Listen for 3 distinct sounds.** It could be the sound of the air conditioner, traffic outside, the sound of typing, or the sound of a bird chirping. Say the three things out loud. Think about where they came from.

- **Identify 2 different smells.** This could be the smell of your coffee, your soap, scented lotion, or the laundry detergent on your clothes.

- **Name 1 thing you can taste.** Notice whatever taste is in your mouth. Is it toothpaste? Coffee? Or try tasting a piece of hard candy.

HOW CAN I INVITE GOD IN? TALK TO GOD.

Our emotions can seem like a complicated mess of conflicting thoughts and feelings that sometimes, as hard as we might try, we can't express or put into words. But the good news is that our Creator already knows what we are going through and what we are feeling so much better than we could ever grasp ourselves. So when it comes to navigating our anxious thoughts and our emotions, our best line of defense is to go straight to God.

The brain-boosting tool God gives us to emotionally exhale is prayer. Prayer is nothing more than talking with God, just like you would talk to a friend. We believe God hears us and already knows our thoughts, so we can be honest and open with Him. He doesn't wait to judge us but listens and responds with love and guidance.

Many people of God have been honest with God about how they feel. King David, who is called a man after God's own heart, wrote down some of his raw, emotion-filled prayers like this one in Psalm 22:1.

> "My God, my God, why have you forsaken me?
> Why are you so far from saving me,
> so far from my cries of anguish?"

The prophet Elijah was honest with God about how weary and tired he felt.[15]

Even Jesus cried out to God in distress as He prayed in the Garden of Gethsemane.[16]

The apostle Paul talked about pleading with God to take away a thorn in his side.[17]

When it comes to anxiety, Paul specifically challenges us to go to God in prayer, letting God know how we feel and what we need. Because ultimately, God is the true source of the calm we so desperately long for. Here's what Paul says:

> "Be anxious for nothing, but in everything by prayer and supplication, with thanksgiving, let your requests be made known to God; and the peace of God, which surpasses all understanding, will guard your hearts and minds through Christ Jesus" (Philippians 3:5, NKJV).

It's okay to be honest with God and tell Him exactly how you feel. Prayer can be a powerful tool to help you process your feelings and emotionally exhale. And as you continue to invite God into your anxiety and rest in the knowledge that He is with you, God will help you experience a peace of mind you won't be able to find on your own.

If you have a hard time focusing when you are trying to pray, try writing down your prayers. Doing this helps you to slow down and reflect. You can use prompts like these:

1. How do I feel physically right now?

2. What's been consuming my thoughts lately?

3. What emotions have I been feeling lately?

4. What does my soul/mind/body need today?

How to Pray

If you're not sure where to start, here is an acronym that helped me pray and have a conversation with God.

CHAT: Confess, Honor, Ask, Thank.

Confess.

Often we think of confession as only admitting things we've done wrong. But confession is more than that. It's about being honest and vulnerable. Confession could be sharing about actions you don't feel good about, thoughts you want to change, or emotions you're feeling. This could look like confessing anger that you would like to let go of. Or asking for forgiveness for something you did that you feel guilt or regret. Or it could be as simple as confessing your need for God and your dependence on Him.

Honor.

Honor means high respect or esteem for someone. To honor God in prayer means to acknowledge who He is in your life. For those of you who have made a commitment to follow Jesus, this looks like praying things like: "God, I acknowledge you are the leader (Lord) of my life." "There is no one greater than you." "God, I choose to worship you."

Ask.

Asking God for something is what we typically think of when we think of prayer. While it's not the only thing we do in talking to God, it's very important to do. Why? Because we need God. So ask Him for help. Ask him for strength, encouragement, guidance, patience, love, and wisdom. God is big enough to handle it all.

Thank.

Thankfulness is a powerful mental health tool, and when we direct that thankfulness to God, it's even more powerful. Thanking God changes our perspective. Gratitude reminds us who is in control and who is the source of the good things in our lives. It reminds us that God is good and despite our circumstances and challenges, there is still something to be thankful for every day.

Recap

It may be tempting for you to try to be strong and not want to be a burden to others, deceiving yourself into thinking that you should ignore your anxiety and that maybe it will just go away. But the reality is that our emotions are going to come out eventually. Stuffing will eventually lead to an emotional implosion or explosion. We can only deal with our emotions when we acknowledge them for what they are.

So don't be afraid to feel your emotions and allow yourself to emotionally exhale. That's one of the most essential steps in breaking the spiral of anxiety. Invite God into the process by talking to Him. Let God know your true feelings. You can be sure that He already understands.

THE LIE
Just ignore it.

THE TRUTH
My emotions matter.

WHAT CAN I DO?
Build healthy habits.

HOW CAN I INVITE GOD IN?
Talk to God.

FOUR

THE LIE: IT'S ALL IN MY HEAD

"I've been staring at my clock for hours. I set my alarm for 5:30 a.m., and in just a few hours, I'm going to have to wake up and face my day. Face . . . those people. My stomach has been in knots all night . . . and whoa, are those hives on my arms? Why is this happening again now?! I'm beyond tired. I was up late finishing up math homework, and now I'm going to have to wake up soon to look over my notes again for the oral part of my Literature class project. Wait, wake up? You'd have to have actually slept to wake up. Ugh."

—Olivia, High School Sophomore, 15

We've all been there—lying awake in the middle of the night, muscles tensing, emotions buzzing, thoughts swarming through our heads, our bodies desperately needing rest. And as hard as we try, we can't fall asleep because we just can't shut off our minds.

Stress is pesky in that it affects almost all of the organs in the human body. Did you know that we can actually feel an emotion, and it shows up in our bodies? Yep. Anxiety can show up with undesirable physical symptoms such as excessive sweating, stomach cramping, vomiting, diarrhea, headaches, muscle tension, and even constipation. These very real physical sensations run counter to the popular belief that anxiety is "all in your head."

THE TRUTH: MY MIND AND BODY ARE CONNECTED

I (Dr. Chinwé) consider myself a "words" girl, and I love the word *synergy*. First, it just sounds cool when it rolls off the tongue. But mostly because of what it means. Synergy refers to the process of things working together to do something better than one thing can do alone.

When it comes to your overall health, you can have *good* synergy, which means your body's organs and systems are working pretty well together. Or, you can have *bad* synergy, in which different organs and systems are basically malfunctioning. We can harness the power of positive synergy just by incorporating a few simple but daily habits.

We hear the phrase "mind over matter." You might be thinking, "I should be able to just power my way through my anxiety through my thinking, right?" That's a popular thought, but the truth is, anxiety is not just in your head; it's physical too. Getting enough good foods, exercise, and sleep all play a part in reducing cortisol levels, those harmful chemicals in your body that are created by stress and anxiety.

Experts in the wellness and nutrition space have long discussed the mind-body connection. Simply put, the mind and body are linked in countless and extraordinary ways. Therefore, one primary way to decrease your anxiety is by taking care of your body. New research shows that taking care of your body helps your brain and your emotions too. So, establishing healthy eating and physical activity habits, particularly when you are young, is important.

Your body is always communicating with you. It will sometimes tell you that you are stressed even if you don't necessarily feel stressed. You've probably experienced stomachaches, headaches, neck, and back aches, but perhaps didn't consider that they were stress-induced. That's why it's important to listen to your body. Paying attention to the signs allows you to intervene before the issue becomes worse.

Here are some subtle ways your body might be telling you that you're stressed, even if you think you aren't:

- Neck and shoulder tension
- Difficulty focusing
- Digestive issues
- Hair loss
- Soreness in your jaw or teeth
- Feeling dehydrated
- Excessive perspiration

Did you know that stress not only feels unpleasant in your body, but it can age you faster? Yikes. It's scary, but it's true. Here's how: Anxiety and fear actually destroy the proteins at the end of our chromosomes. Destroying anything inside of your body is definitely not a good idea, but in this case, destroying these proteins dramatically increases the aging process. And who wants to get old faster than they already are? I can't think of a more compelling reason to reduce stress and fear.

WHAT CAN I DO? BUILD HEALTHY HABITS

Many aspects of our human existence are beyond our control, and there will *always* be stress-inducing events and people that are *completely* out of our control (for example, traffic, mean people, our calculus teacher, a global health pandemic). Still, we *do* have some control over how well we take care of ourselves.

In the past several years, I (Dr. Chinwé) have noticed that self-care has become a buzzword, especially among social media influencers. And I'm fine with it because it's a legitimate practice for your overall health and well-being. As a clinical therapist, my job goes beyond supporting my clients when they struggle emotionally. Another very important part of my role is prevention.

Promoting healthful eating and exercise habits has been part of my psychological arsenal for years. Why? Because it is effective for the mind *and* the body. A healthful lifestyle contributes to a healthy brain, which helps minimize stress and anxiety.

How Can I Take Care of My Body?

One of the best ways to counteract the effects of stress and to reduce the negative self-talk that often comes along with stress is to take good care of your *physical* self before the stress gets out of control.

Simply put, when you feel better, you think better.

One of the very first things I advise my clients to do is to take an honest look at the foods they eat and how much sleep and movement they get. Eating well, getting enough rest, and regular exercise will go a long way toward strengthening your ability to adapt to stress and reduce the toll of negative emotions like stress, anxiety, or panic. **Practicing these healthy habits alone can reduce the effects of anxiety, even without medication or therapy.**

I know, I know, you already know you should eat healthfully and exercise; you've heard it a million times. But I just want you to hear it once again from me, your therapist friend, because we can't say it or hear it enough. Please don't miss the crucial role it plays in managing your anxiety.

Let's break it down with a few self-care habits you can work on starting today that will help you combat your anxiety.

Habit #1: Feed Your Brain

What's food got to do with it?

Quick question. Do you eat for fun, or do you eat for fuel? Your body needs food for energy to fuel the cells in your body. Because as a young person, your brain is developing so rapidly, it needs all of the energy and metabolic resources that a healthy and balanced diet provides. What we put into our bodies matters for every aspect of health, including mental and emotional health.[21] **It can change things, sometimes dramatically.**

So, even though a daily rotation of pizza and cheeseburgers paired with your favorite soda might be more "comforting" or convenient in the moment, opting for more fruits and vegetables, fish, and whole grains can actually help you fight off anxiety and despair. That's not to mention the improvements in your physical health too.

Whole foods, including healthy fats, provide many benefits to your mental health, both short-term and long-term, so it's really worth making an effort to incorporate them into your diet. And eating enough food is just as important as the kinds of foods you choose to eat.

You may not have 100 percent control of your diet or the kinds of foods you are able to consume. We get it! Healthier foods can sometimes be more expensive, and you may not always have access to them, especially if you have to rely on the selection at the school cafeteria. But even a few small changes, like opting for a bowl of fruit instead of a bag of chips, can have a major impact on your mental health.[22]

7 Foods That Can Help Fight Anxiety

 Salmon and other fatty fish have omega 3s and vitamin D, which help reduce inflammation and improve mental health. Get in at least two servings a week.

 Organic poultry is high in protein and tryptophan and balances blood sugar.

 Eggs are a good source of protein, tryptophan, and vitamin D.

 Pumpkin seeds are rich in magnesium and antioxidants.

 Dark chocolate contains flavonoids and magnesium and produces serotonin, the "happy" chemical, and it tastes so good! Limit to a 1-1.5 ounce serving.

 Green tea contains theanine which is soothing and may relieve anxiety.

 Organic fruits and leafy greens have higher levels of beneficial compounds.[22] Leafy veggies like spinach contain vitamin C and folate which produces dopamine, the happy chemical.

3 Vitamins to Help Fight Anxiety

I don't know about you, but I've always hated taking vitamins. What if I told you they are another important tool to help you battle your anxiety? These are the simple nutrients your body needs that you may not be getting if you're not intentional about it. It's always better to get your vitamins and nutrients from your food, but sometimes, supplements are necessary. Magnesium, Zinc, and Vitamin D are a few vitamins you can focus on getting more of if you are dealing with anxiety. Be sure to consult with your doctor before adding supplements or making any significant changes to your diet.

 Magnesium calms the brain and body. A deficiency in this vitamin may be contributing to your anxiety. You can find magnesium in foods like nuts (almonds), whole cereals, fruits, green leafy vegetables (spinach and collards), and dark chocolate.

 Zinc supports brain function and helps reduce symptoms of anxiety for some people. You can find zinc in foods like red meat (opt for grass-fed beef and lamb when possible), shellfish, legumes, seeds, and nuts.

 Vitamin D: A healthy dose of sun exposure can improve your body and your mind and plays an important role in regulating mood and decreasing depression. But you can also find vitamin D in foods like salmon, canned tuna, trout, mushrooms, fortified cereals, and orange juice.

When you're stressed out, do you crave *anything but* healthy foods? If so, you probably crave sugary, processed, or so-called "comfort foods." You're not alone. A lot of us do.[24] Part of the reason is that eating helps distract us from our stress, at least temporarily. But the reality is it does more harm than good. Emotional eating has been linked to obesity and a lack of motivation. And it can actually increase your anxiety.[25]

So when you think about choosing food to help you feel better, especially when you are stressed, pause and ask yourself, "What can I eat right now that will help *reduce* my anxiety and *not fuel* it?"

Foods That Can Fuel Anxiety

While symptoms and triggers are different for everyone, nutritional studies have found several foods that can induce anxiety and even panic.

Processed Foods

Processed and refined foods are often stripped of essential nutrients. The foods that are widely available in today's Standard American Diet (SAD), particularly those high in sugar and refined carbs, break down and release sugar molecules and elevate your blood sugar. Chronically elevated blood sugar causes insulin spikes which have been found to contribute to a higher risk of anxiety and depression.

These foods include:
- ▸ Packaged and processed bakery products
- ▸ Doughnuts
- ▸ Foods marketed as "healthy" like granola bars and energy bars
- ▸ Fried foods
- ▸ Refined cereals

Sugar

According to nutritionists, we are a culture that is highly addicted to sugar. Did you know that just *anticipating* your favorite dessert (mine are Cinnabons®) can increase the release of dopamine and trigger the reward pathway in the brain? That process makes it harder to resist those yummy sweets. Sugar is in everything, so it's impossible to avoid altogether, but it can be reduced, especially when you are aware that it can contribute to your anxiety. Again, it all has to do with your blood sugar levels. When you eat something sweet, your blood sugar spikes and then later crashes, which can cause a spike in your anxiety. Sugar, in moderation, is fine. But it's easy to experience sugar overload.

Caffeine

Coffee, the drink that helps us wake up and get through our day, can also be a drag when you have anxiety. But not for everyone. The jury is mixed on caffeine. One study found that moderate caffeine intake in the form of coffee may actually reduce anxiety and decrease symptoms of depression due to caffeine's *combined* stimulant effect and antioxidant properties. However, other studies suggest that caffeine may increase symptoms of anxiety and depression among teenagers.

I know, it can be a bit confusing. But since teenagers are the fastest growing population of caffeine users, let's focus on the effects of overconsumption of caffeine on a teenage mind and body. Studies show that teens who drink more than four cups of coffee (or a caffeinated alternative) are more likely to have poor concentration, sleep, and mood.[26]

Energy drinks can be even more problematic due to their high levels of both caffeine *and* sugar. If you are experiencing anxiety as a teenager or young adult, start by eliminating caffeine altogether—especially if you are having a hard time sleeping at night.

Alcohol

Did you know drinking alcohol can trigger anxiety? Alcohol is linked to both depression and anxiety. We know that some people drink as a way to cope with severe anxiety or depression, but alcohol can actually trigger new anxiety and depressive episodes.

The reason is that alcohol is a depressant. (It's actually both a depressant and a stimulant. I'll explain more about that later.) Alcohol slows down your brain and nervous system processes, which can feel cool at first because initially you feel more relaxed and less inhibited,[27] but be aware, those effects don't last long. In fact, if you have anxiety, alcohol could be making your symptoms worse.

Here's the simplified version of how it works: the more alcohol you consume over time, your central nervous system adjusts to the suppressing effects. So, if the alcohol levels all of a sudden drop (because, let's say, you aren't drinking at the same level), your nervous system goes into a fight-or-flight state—the same brain state that is associated with anxiety and fear.[28]

Tips for Cutting Back on Alcohol

Okay, so we know that the legal drinking age in the US is 21, but we also know that some teens and young adults have been known to experiment with alcohol. And others, well, they do more than just experiment. We are not here to judge you. However, if you've been struggling with your anxiety and have been known to consume alcohol occasionally, try cutting back.

Need some guidance on how? Here's a four-step plan.

1. **Track** how much alcohol you drink. Use an app designed to track drinking or other eating habits.

2. **Reduce** your intake gradually.

3. **Maintain.** Once you've cut back (or stopped altogether), try to maintain it for at least two weeks. Most people see a reduction in anxiety symptoms at this point as their brains balance out. You might even notice improved sleep!

4. **Assess.** Continue to assess your anxiety symptoms. If you still experience the same rate of anxiety, contact your doctor or a mental health therapist for support. (There's more on how to locate a therapist in chapter 7.

Even the small steps you take today to fuel your body in the right way can have a noticeable impact on your emotional and mental well-being. Because your anxiety isn't all in your head, your mind and body are connected.

Habit #2: Get Some Rest

According to a new study, **the strongest predictor of mental well-being is the amount of quality sleep you get.**[29]

Perhaps you're someone who is juggling classes, trying to complete homework at a decent hour, maybe working a part-time or full-time job, and participating in sports or other extracurricular activities. In many cases, sleep can easily get crowded out. It's normal for sleep patterns to change as you age. For instance, sleep patterns shift in adolescence due to changes in your circadian rhythm. You may notice that you are staying up later and sleeping in longer. That's completely normal. And if you didn't have anxiety, that would be just fine.

But as most people with anxiety will tell you, anxiety can feel like your thoughts are racing a mile a minute, and your heart is right there competing with it, which can feel mentally and physically exhausting! So, getting enough sleep is important.

What's the Big Deal About Sleep?

This one is easy. Sleep is a time for your body and brain to repair.

For your brain to function optimally, you need both focus and rest. Rest is critical for all of us, and this is especially true for teenagers. **Teenagers need about eight to ten hours of sleep per night.**

When you switch off our "focus" brain, it will automatically link ideas, retrieve memories, and enable you to become more creative. Rest doesn't have to happen at night. So, start now to build those unfocused times throughout your day. Resting, sleeping, reflecting, and napping are activities that keep the creative juices flowing, which in turn stimulates the brain.

Not getting enough sleep increases levels of the stress hormone cortisol and over time exaggerates your response to stress, which can have a negative impact on your school performance and mood.

Essentially, not getting enough sleep leads to the following:

- ▸ Recurrent negative thoughts
- ▸ Rumination (repeatedly thinking about the same thoughts)
- ▸ Excessive worry
- ▸ Over-magnification of problems
- ▸ Feelings of helplessness

Do you know how when your phone starts glitching or your computer freezes up, sometimes the only way to fix it is to shut it down and reboot? In the same way, when you're stressed out and feeling anxious, you might need to just reboot (that is, get some sleep).

Of course, I know what you're probably thinking: "Thanks for the advice, Dr. Chinwé. I'd love to go to sleep, but I just can't! I'm too anxious!" Falling asleep and staying asleep is no easy task when you are a busy student and you are feeling stressed. Check out some quick tips on the next page that might help:

Tips for a Good Night's Sleep

- Say no to caffeine after noon.

- Try to get schoolwork done by a certain time each night.

- Try not to do aerobic exercise within two hours of your bedtime.

- Avoid alcohol. While alcohol is technically a depressant, when it's first ingested, it acts a lot like a stimulant because alcohol triggers the brain to release dopamine, which is a neurotransmitter that provides energy and stimulation.

- Keep your bedroom cool and dark by using lights minimally or not at all.

- Limit or cut off screens (computers, TVs, phones) at a certain hour.

- If you feel restless and are having trouble falling asleep, get out of bed and do some light activity or read (not on a digital device) in bed until you feel more sleepy.

- Limit daytime napping if you have trouble sleeping at night.

Relaxation exercises help to calm anxious thoughts and promote sleepiness. Having trouble falling asleep? Try progressive muscle relaxation, which helps to release muscle tension in your body.

Here's how to practice progressive muscle relaxation: beyondthespiralbook.com

Habit #3: Get Moving

There's no better way to get the mind and body working together to improve your mental state than when you get your body moving. When I was in counseling graduate school, I had a professor who was also a successful private practice clinician. He would flat-out refuse to treat any patients with mild or moderate anxiety or depression *unless* they signed an agreement stating they would walk for thirty minutes at least three times per week before starting therapy.

Initially, I thought to myself, "Isn't that rather harsh? People are coming to you for help, and you're telling them to literally first take a stroll?" I didn't get it at first. Years later, I started implementing movement as a part of many of my clients' treatment plans and noticed improvements in their anxiety and overall quality of life.

In this era of fancy digital devices that are widely promoted to reduce anxiety (from meditation headbands to stress relief bracelets), let me be clear, nothing compares to simply getting active! Movement is one of the first interventions I recommend to my clients struggling with anxiety because it's free, usually convenient, and offers the most bang for your buck.

Let me acknowledge something. I know you are busy, and the thought of adding one more thing to your already full plate may be nauseating. However . . .

Hands down, exercise is one of the best things you can do to combat stress.

As we mentioned in chapter 1, hormones like cortisol and adrenaline are really helpful for navigating a dangerous situation. But a continuous release of those hormones causes us to stay on edge. Because anxiety is also physical, doing something physical helps release those hormones and complete the cycle of stress, which helps you feel better.[30]

One of the most powerful methods for reducing anxiety is vigorous movement. I know it may seem paradoxical, but placing (good) physical stress on your body can actually decrease mental stress in your brain. You might be asking, "How is that?" For starters, exercise is a natural outlet for your body when it is in the fight-flight-freeze defense mode. Also, movement supports thinking.

Aerobic Exercise

Aerobic exercise can help key regions of the brain to connect better. It also improves concentration and focus. Have you ever heard someone say, "I am going for a run to clear my head"? If you are preparing for a job or scholarship interview, or even a final exam, try walking or running around the block for about twenty minutes while going over your notes! It really does help.

Just 120 minutes of aerobic exercise per week can help your memory and verbal learning. And, finally, if you're an overthinker and chronic worrier, exercise can help you sleep better at night.

Walking

If you're brand new to fitness or have been away from it for a while, begin with walking. Walking has many advantages over other types of exercise. First, there's no equipment required other than a decent pair of walking shoes. Additionally, walking alone has been proven to boost creative thinking.

Weights

Strength-building or "heavy muscle" tasks can release chemicals called endorphins that also help decrease anxiety. The other day, my friend shared a video that offered a really cool way to think about how strength training helps us to reduce stress and anxiety. When you contract your muscles, it secretes these proteins into your bloodstream that some call "hope molecules."[31] These molecules go through your bloodstream and travel to your brain and help you become resilient to stress. How cool is that? Here are some activities that help us contract muscles:

- Lifting weights
- Using resistance bands
- Sit-ups
- Push-ups
- Shoveling snow
- Pushing a wheelbarrow
- Stacking wood
- Digging while gardening
- Hiking

Weights are also used with what we call pressure therapy. Applying calm pressure to your body activates your parasympathetic nervous system which lowers your heart rate when you're stressed. Try some pressure therapy by:

- Wearing a weighted vest
- Walking with ankle weights
- Snuggling under a weighted or a heavy blanket

Find the activity that moves you.

There are many things you can do to engage your body. What it boils down to is this: Any physical activity like running, biking, roller-blading, dancing, or even walking the dog regularly for just a few minutes per day helps your brain. Movement provides mental and emotional relief by lowering cortisol levels (your body's stress hormones) and releasing endorphins (your brain's feel-good chemicals).

Remember, God made your body, mind, and spirit to be connected. **So listen to your body. It may be talking to you.** Here are some surprising signs your body may be telling you that you're not moving enough:

- You're more constipated than usual.
- Your joints feel stiff.
- You constantly feel out of breath.
- You're feeling irritable, anxious, or moody.
- You feel tired even though you sleep well.
- You keep forgetting things.

Habit #4: Get Outside

While eating right, sleeping enough, and getting moving are the three most important things you can do to take care of your body, doing any of those things outside takes it up a notch.

Nature Is Healing

As it turns out, being in nature is *really* good for our mental health. Research suggests that simple changes in how we relate to God's creation—plants, animals, landscapes, and other natural elements—can profoundly affect our moods and relationships.

There is now an entire field of therapy called ecotherapy dedicated to the various methods that reconnect us to the healing capacities of nature.

And as a side note, eco-anxiety is real. If you sometimes feel anxious about the state of the world and climate destruction and habitat loss, you're not alone. I believe that our disconnection from nature, and green space specifically, is another source of our nation's collective anxiety.

But here's the point: Too much time indoors can make us sick. So, get outside!

Sunshine Is Healing

Decreased sun exposure has been linked to lower serotonin levels, which can lead to depression. Have you ever noticed a shift in your mood as the season transitioned from summer to fall? Many people experience this type of depression in winter, especially as the days get shorter.

Remember we called vitamin D the sunshine vitamin? There's a reason for that. Many studies point to low vitamin D levels as a risk factor for anxiety.[32,33,34] Vitamin D is one of those anxiety-busting, mood-boosting vitamins we mentioned earlier in this section. Your body naturally produces vitamin D with direct sun exposure. According to the World Health Organization (WHO), anywhere between **five to fifteen minutes of sun exposure** on your arms, hands, and face, two to three times a week, can boost vitamin D.

Because excessive sun exposure is linked with skin cancer, if you're going to be outside for more than fifteen minutes, use sunscreen with an SPF of at least fifteen.

Do you live in a region that doesn't get a lot of sun? Or will you be stuck with cold, dark, or cloudy conditions for more than a week? Consider purchasing a light lamp. These have been shown to provide benefits similar to the sun. Be sure to consult with your doctor.

Some things to consider:

- How much time do you spend outdoors?

- What aspects of nature are you naturally drawn to?

- Bring natural elements inside, like plants, artwork, fountains, and anything that can connect you to nature.

- Try gardening. Did you know soil bacteria boosts mood? I knew someone who really enjoyed gardening. The more she gardened, the less she needed her anxiety medication.

Getting Into Nature Exercise

Here's a quick exercise when you're feeling anxious and want to get out in nature.

- Find somewhere you can relax out in nature, either sitting or standing.

- Drop your shoulders.

- Notice your bottom in your chair or your feet on the floor/ground.

- Notice your breath.

- Be sure to notice the rise and fall of your breath.

- When you're outside or when you're looking out a window, what direction are you facing?

- What does the sky look like?

- What is the position of the sun?

- How many things can you identify that are the color green? What about orange or brown? Notice the clouds, the wind.

- Now, notice your internal state.

- If a thought pops up, notice it.

- Don't pay attention to the thoughts in detail.

- Let them scroll by; do not cling to them or reject them. Just notice them.

Quiz

How Well Are You Taking Care of Yourself?

Read through each question carefully and circle Yes or No.

1. Do you have a morning routine that includes **Yes   No** healthy habits (like not immediately reaching for the phone) and allows you to start your day with some time for you?

2. Do you engage in a regular practice of deep **Yes   No** breathing?

3. Do you have a few minutes of time alone every day? **Yes   No**

4. Do you eat fairly healthy (primarily non-processed **Yes   No** foods) most days per week?

5. Do you exercise (or engage in some movement **Yes   No** for thirty minutes) most days of the week?

6. Do you have hobbies, interests, or outlets that you **Yes   No** are passionate about?

7. Do you take breaks while you're studying or work- **Yes   No** ing to check in with how you are feeling?

8. Do you have people who you can talk to that really **Yes   No** hear you?

9. Do you eat regularly (more than one meal per day)? **Yes   No**

10. Do you stop and go to the bathroom right when **Yes   No** you need to?

11. Do you say no when you don't want to do **Yes   No** something?

12. Do you have a peaceful place in your home that **Yes No** you can go to unwind from your school or work day? A room, a couch, a corner, or a deck?

13. Do you have time in the evening to read, listen **Yes No** to music, play with your pet, get out in nature, or something else you enjoy doing to unwind?

14. Do you spend time with friends who really get you **Yes No** and have the same interests and values as you?

15. Do you have a nighttime ritual of letting your body **Yes No** know it is time to settle down and get ready for sleep? Does this routine include turning off all electronics at least an hour before bed, and turning down lights and noise?

16. Do you sleep at least eight hours a night? **Yes No**

17. Do you have a regular bedtime and wake-up time? **Yes No**

18. Do you take care of your basic needs? Hydrate, **Yes No** eat when hungry, and walk or stretch when your body feels tense?

19. Do you have any spiritual routines that nourish **Yes No** you (prayer, Scripture reading, gratitude journal, attending church or small group, walking in nature, or something else)?

20. Do you acknowledge and express your emotions, **Yes No** including anger and sadness?

....

Figuring Out Your Self-Care Score

_____ **Number of Total Yeses**

1-5: You are in need of more self-care. Remember, self-care is not selfish! It's important to take the time to do healthy things for yourself. Consider adding in some of the nutritional, emotional, and mental wellness tips mentioned in this book, then retake this quiz in two weeks.

6-10: You may be vulnerable to feelings of stress and overwhelm. Try not to over-exert yourself. Consider adding in some of the nutritional, emotional, and mental wellness tips mentioned in this book.

11-15: Congratulations! You are engaging in some wellness practices, and that is terrific. If you are still experiencing some anxiety, consider if there are still some areas that you might want to work on. Look at the no's and see what areas stand out.

16-20: AWESOME! You are doing a fantastic job prioritizing your wellness. Keep up the great work!

....

We can't stress this enough. The way you treat your body has a major effect on your ability to fight off the stress and anxiety that you are confronted with on a daily basis because your mind and your body are connected. So choose good foods, get moving outside, and get plenty of sleep. Both your body and your brain will thank you for it.

HOW CAN I INVITE GOD IN? GROW IN SELF-CONTROL

The Word of God reminds us that our bodies are temples. Paul tells us in a letter to the Corinthians,

> "Do you not know that your bodies are temples of the Holy Spirit, who is in you, whom you have received from God? You are not your own" (1 Corinthians 6:19, NIV).

Focus on fueling your body the way God intended. Our bodies are connected to our minds, and our minds are connected to our souls. It's all connected. God cares about you . . . all of you. He wants the best for you. Since the beginning, God has been directing us with what is best for us and has already provided us with everything our bodies need and were created for.

So with God's help, what can you do? Grow in self-control.

Self-control isn't just powering through the will of the mind. Having self-control is spiritual. It is a result of following God's lead.

> "For God has not given us a spirit of fear but of power, love and self-control" (2 Timothy 1:7, NIV).

Though showing self-control on our own can prove difficult, with the power of God's Spirit working within us, we can gain control over desires that are harmful, allowing us to stay in line with what is best for us and live the healthy life He created us for.

So How Can I Grow in Self-Control?

Ask God for help.

Acknowledge your dependence and need for His help. If you have an addiction or habit you are trying to control, start by admitting it to God. If you have a leader or a small group that you trust, talk to them as well. You cannot change what you do not acknowledge. Whenever I (Will) wanted to change something in my life or grow in self-control, I started by acknowledging it. As a young adult, admitting that I was drinking to cope with stress was the first step in breaking that habit. Admitting my fear and worry after my panic attack was the first step in changing my pace. Acknowledging that drinking caffeine in the afternoon wasn't the best for my body was the first step to making changes.

With God's help, work on habit-breaking and habit-building.

In his book *Atomic Habits*, James Clear talks about four ways to build good habits and four ways to break bad habits. To build good habits, Clear says to make the thing you want to do obvious, attractive, easy, and satisfying.[35]

For instance, if you want to get more sleep, make it easier and more obvious to your brain by doing things that slow your mind down before bedtime. Or, if you want to exercise more, put your exercise gear right by your bed, plan a time that is easy for you, and make it attractive and satisfying by doing something you think is fun. If you like playing soccer but hate lifting weights, then do the more attractive activity.

To break bad habits, Clear says to make those activities: invisible, unattractive, hard, and unsatisfying. If you want to drink less caffeine, only drink black coffee for a little while. If you have a bad habit of staying up too late, make staying up harder by setting a timer on your internet that someone else has the password to.

Practice Moderation.

Moderation is a common theme in Scripture. Moderation avoids extremes and embraces limits. Even good things for our bodies can be bad things if we have too much. Like the proverb says, "It is not good to eat too much honey" (Proverbs 25:27, NIV). Too much of anything, either good or bad, can be harmful. Moderation helps us to make wise choices with our food and activities.

Take some time to write down a response to the following questions:

What's one practical action I can do today to improve my anxiety?

_____

_____

_____

_____

What area(s) in my life do I need to set some limits and practice moderation?

_____

_____

_____

_____

Who is someone I can tell about my new habit who will also encourage me to keep doing it?

_____

_____

_____

_____

Recap

Synergy is the reason why the small, routine things we do daily—and probably take for granted—make a difference in our emotional and mental health and overall well-being. But, it starts with intentional lifestyle habits focused on self-care. Getting good nutrition, sleep, exercise, and getting in nature are all key components to improved mental health and reduced anxiety. Invite God to help you take care of yourself by allowing Him to empower you with His Spirit and equip you with inner strength so that you can grow in self-control in all of these areas.

THE LIE
It's all in my head.

THE TRUTH
My mind and body are connected.

WHAT CAN I DO?
Build healthy habits.

HOW CAN I INVITE GOD IN?
Grow in self-control.

FIVE

THE LIE:
I HAVE NO CONTROL

'"What if I hate my school? What if I don't make any friends? What if I try out for the team and embarrass myself? What if something terrible happens to my parents, and I suddenly become alone in a new city? I won't be able to make it on my own. None of this is going to work out for me, so what's the point?'

All of these thoughts were constantly swirling around my head. I had just moved to Atlanta from Indiana and was about to start a new school. I was so anxious about my new situation that it landed me in a therapist's office, especially after the panic attacks started. Honestly, I just felt completely out of control. I felt helpless, vulnerable, and fearful about everything.

I would often stay up late, restless and scrolling through my phone, only to wake up hours later with another attack, leaving me feeling miserable most mornings. Sometimes I just felt like life was not worth living. Dr. Chinwé helped me log some of my pretty wild thoughts, which showed me the source of all my fears and how surprisingly angry I was at my parents for moving."

—Lisa, High School Junior, 16

Have you ever had a thought and then thought to yourself, "Wait, where in the world did that come from?" As it turns out, we have a lot of random thoughts per day. And when we feel anxious, our thoughts tend to be more negative, more catastrophic, and involve a lot of worries about future events. Anxious thoughts can make us feel like we have no control. Have you ever felt this way?

Why do I feel out of control?

Worry makes us feel out of control for many reasons. For starters, anxiety triggers your body's stress response system, which actually affects your concentration and the short-term learning areas of your brain.

When you're having trouble focusing, it takes much longer to complete a task—even something routine or mundane. And when you are having trouble concentrating, it can take longer to complete a pre-calculus equation or even read a short chapter. When I (Dr. Chinwé) am feeling anxious, it could take me close to twenty minutes to craft a simple three-sentence email. So, think about how anxiety affects you during a presentation or a major midterm exam.

Anxiety also feels out of control because we are constantly planning, anticipating, preparing (and sometimes avoiding) future events that may or may not occur. That's the funny thing; most of what we worry about, like 90%, doesn't happen. **We think we are managing our worries by worrying, but we are just *looping our worries.***

Anxiety can feel exhausting because there are literally a billion things we could imagine disappointing us or going wrong. And our minds tend to replay those scenarios over and over again. Experts call this the *worry spiral.*

You may not realize it, but there's almost always a trigger that sets off the spiral. **A trigger is anything, internal or external, that leads to what-if scenarios and questions.**

Here is an example of some triggers and associated what-if/worry questions. Additional boxes are left open for you to use with a counselor or a friend.

Triggering Event	What if Question
Not getting invited to a friend's party.	What if she thinks I am too awkward or embarrassing?
Mom left the house to run an errand and is gone for a much longer period of time than expected.	What if something terrible happened to her?
You see an unexplained rash on your arm.	What if this is a symptom of a major illness? What if I'm dying?
You realize you forgot a class assignment at home.	What if I forgot something else? Did I remember to turn the stove off?

A PDF of this can be found at beyondthespiralbook.com.

Triggering Event	What if Question

Once you've discovered your triggers and then the corresponding what-if/worry question, you'll want to replace your unhelpful thoughts with more positive or neutral ones.

But first, begin to notice how those thoughts can be so distorted that they cause you to behave in a certain way that can make things worse and even impact your overall mental health.

THE TRUTH: I CAN CHANGE MY THOUGHTS

One of the biggest lies we hear about anxiety, in particular, is that we have no control. But there's good news. You have some control. There are a few things you *can* change that will impact the way you feel, like the way you take care of your body (which we've already talked about in the previous chapter) but also in the way you think. You see, it's not *all* in your head, but some of it is.

Pause for a second. What are you thinking about right now? Growing up, my mom often said, "An idle mind is the devil's workshop." I always thought this was her way of getting me to clean my room or help her with dinner when I just wanted to sit around and do absolutely nothing. Maybe.

But the truth is our thoughts and beliefs do have a strong influence on our actions. Cognitive behavioral therapists believe that it is not the *event* that causes stress and worry but our *interpretation* of the event. In other words, **what you *think* about a situation that happens to you really matters, and it matters much more than the actual situation.**

So, *change your thoughts!* It's that easy, right? Not so fast. Some thoughts are easier to change than others.

- "I just failed that science test . . . even after studying. I'm such an idiot."

- "Mom hasn't texted back yet. It's been more than fifteen minutes. She probably got into a car accident and is badly hurt."

- "I'm always the last one to be chosen for anything. No one thinks I'm good at anything."

- "I haven't been on one date. No one has even expressed interest. No one likes me. I'm such a loser."

- "If I didn't have bad luck, then I wouldn't have any luck at all."

- "This always happens to me; I never catch a break."

Any of these sound familiar? These are pretty good examples of what are known as cognitive distortions.

Cognitive distortions are habitual and typically negative thought patterns that cause us to view ourselves, others, and situations in inaccurate (and typically negative) ways.

The human brain does a lot of thinking. Some studies estimate on the low end that humans have 6,200 thoughts per day. But some say it's actually closer to 60,000. Wow. That's a lot of thinking! And the majority of those thoughts (almost 90%) aren't pretty. They are negative and repetitive.

Have you ever had what some call a "thoughtmare"? It's like a nightmare, but you are awake the whole time. It's when your brain takes you to the worst-case scenario, and suddenly you are planning your funeral because you Googled the causes of a racing heart.

Everyone's imagination does this. Most of us experience negative or terrifying thoughts from time to time. While the tendency to exaggerate is something we all occasionally do, cognitive distortions are sneaky and persistent. They convince you of something that isn't true.

Over time, repetitive negative thinking and self-talk can change the hardwiring of your brain. If reinforced frequently enough, it increases anxiety, sadness, and even deep depression.

Some other effects on your brain and body include:

▸ Feeling overwhelmed and exhausted
▸ Constantly in survival (fight-or-flight) mode
▸ Feeling stuck or numb
▸ Increased symptoms of depression
▸ Chronic stress
▸ Damaged immune system
▸ Uncontrollable inflammation

Our thinking is *very* different when we're feeling anxious. **Anxious thoughts can be gloomy, pessimistic, and can multiply pretty quickly. Sort of like an ant infestation.**

Have you ever seen a solo ant wandering around? You think he's harmless until you notice he's brought a few friends, and before you know it, there's an unending stream of ants stumbling all over each other in each direction, blindly following the path set before them. If only you had squashed that solo ant when you had the chance.

Negative thoughts work in a similar way. Neuroscientist and psychiatrist Dr. Daniel Amen popularized the term ANTS (automatic negative thoughts) in his bestselling book, *Change Your Brain, Change Your Body.*[36] As the story goes, Dr. Amen was in medical school and came home frustrated after a long and exhausting day of working with his patients. Dr. Amen was ready to hang up his jacket and kick his shoes off to relax, only to discover *thousands* of ants crawling around his kitchen. As he was angrily cleaning up the swarm of ants, he began to associate the negative thoughts taking over the brains of his patients with the ant infestation occurring in his kitchen. That, my friends, is how an acronym was born: automatic negative thoughts (ANTs). As a result of this new insight, Dr. Amen then began teaching his patients how to get rid of all of the ANTs that were robbing them of peace, confidence, and joy.

Anxiety is indeed tricky and deceptive. It can trick your mind into thinking that those scary future-oriented thoughts are accurate, but the truth is they only serve to reinforce other negative thoughts until they become automatic and your default mode, and you have an infestation of ANTs.

Repetitive negative thoughts, left unchecked, can lead to chronic stress. Chronic stress can stem from many of the sources we've talked about so far, such as suppressed emotions, environment (toxins or toxic people), what you eat, and how much sleep you get. But limiting negative thoughts or beliefs you have about yourself and others has a major impact on your mental and physical health. In her book, *Switch on Your Brain,* Dr. Caroline Leaf shared that **75 percent to 98 percent of mental, physical, and behavioral illnesses come from our thought life**.[37] In addition, medical research estimates as much as **90 percent of illnesses and diseases are stress-related.** Due to those pretty extreme consequences, it's important to eradicate those ANTS. The good news is there are many ways you can release or adapt to the causes of stress in your life.

Thanks to pioneers in the field of psychology, such as Dr. Aaron Beck, who is widely regarded as the "father of cognitive therapy," we now know that negative thinking can quickly spiral us into states of anxiety and depression.

But there's good news. We have also learned proven ways to reduce or "exterminate" those pesky thoughts!

WHAT CAN I DO? REFRAME NEGATIVE THOUGHTS

By now, you probably realize that those negative thoughts pop up automatically and are quite harmful if left unchecked. Remember Lisa from the beginning of this chapter? Her thoughts were pretty negative, which increased her anxiety and feelings of fear and dread.

Let's take a look at what happens in the brain again. As you might remember from your biology or psychology class, the brain is made up of neurons (nerve cells), which are the basic building blocks of the brain and nervous system. We have about 100 billion neurons that send and receive information throughout the entire human body. Neurons transmit information between the brain and the rest of the nervous system.

The neural pathways in our brains light up when we think of something for the first time, like something as simple as an orange or even more complex topics such as forgiveness, justice, or love. Neural pathways strengthen and develop based on use.

Have you ever heard of the phrase, "Neurons that fire together wire together"? This phrase basically reminds us that when we repeat an experience (like a thought) over and over, the brain learns to trigger the same neurons each time.

In other words: **The more you think certain thoughts, the more of those types of thoughts you think.**

Thanks to research on neuroplasticity, we know we can retrain our brains! Neuroplasticity is the brain's ability to constantly change by creating new neural pathways and getting rid of those which are no longer needed or used.

So, you might be wondering, is there something I can do to change the way my brain works so I don't have as much anxiety? Absolutely. There are many things you can do. You can rewire your brain by building new thought habits that generate more peace, calm, and joy.[38] As you practice sending your thoughts down new pathways, you weaken the old ones and strengthen new ones.

What Are Thought Exercises?

Thought exercises offer new ways to think about a given situation or experience that can help you to get out of a stuck or unhelpful thought pattern.

The following strategies will help you reprogram *unhelpful* thought patterns by examining your anxious thoughts and then exchanging them for helpful and productive thoughts. These are the same strategies I (Dr. Chinwé) use with my clients with an approach called cognitive behavioral therapy (CBT).

It's important to note that there isn't a one-size-fits-all strategy. Try one of them for about two weeks and observe how it impacts your anxiety and overall mental health. If it works, fantastic! If not, you can try a different one.

Many of my clients have discovered two things by using these strategies: Change *is* possible, and results are quicker than they ever imagined. Working through these methods—over time—ultimately left them feeling more confident and much more in control.

Step #1: Write Down Thoughts and Triggers

One of the best ways to recognize anxious thoughts is to write them down. Writing our thoughts is beneficial because our memories are short and may not accurately represent what we actually worry about. We recommend keeping a thought or worry log to track both **triggering events,** and subsequent **what-if worry thoughts.**

Here are some examples of **triggers and worries:**

What triggered me?

- ▸ I felt unsafe.
- ▸ I felt unheard.
- ▸ I felt blamed.
- ▸ I felt helpless.
- ▸ I felt controlled.
- ▸ I felt criticized.
- ▸ I felt invisible or unseen.

Worry list

- ▸ I'm going to vomit.
- ▸ I'm going to forget my lines.
- ▸ My throat will close up as soon as I open my mouth.
- ▸ My friend will reject me, and I'll be all alone.

You can practice doing a few of these in the chart on page 96.

Step #2: Find an Alternative Explanation

Once you've thought through your triggers and worries, now comes the most important step. Come up with an alternate explanation. What might seem true may not be really true. So what are some true things that you can hold on to when your thoughts begin to spiral? These thoughts can keep you grounded.

Alternative explanations

- My anxiety makes me feel like I will vomit, but I rarely or ever have.

- I'm well prepared, and if I forget a word or two, no one will ever notice.

- My vocal and breathing exercises will help warm up my mouth and relax my throat.

- I'm not alone. I have friends in my neighborhood and small group who enjoy spending time with me.

When we have negative thoughts, we usually dwell on the information that confirms our conclusions. To exterminate the ANTs (automatic negative thoughts), we must examine the evidence. If you temporarily suspend your belief that your worries are true or your worst fears will occur, you will find it easier to find contradictory evidence that weakens your conclusion.

Counter your thoughts with questions like these:

- Am I completely sure _____ will happen?

- What is the probability that _____ will happen? *Is it 60%? 100%? Or 30%?*

- Has it ever happened before?

- If it does happen, what is the worst thing that will happen?

- Can I live through it?

- Would I be able to cope?

- Who would help me to cope?

- Have I coped with something remotely similar before?

An example of a completed thought record with thoughts, triggers and alternative explanations is below, as well as some blank boxes for your own use or to use with a friend.

A PDF of the worksheet on the next pages is available at beyondthespiralbook.com

Reframing Exercise

Thought	Trigger (Event or Situation)	Alternative Explanations
"I have no real friends."	"I sat alone in the cafeteria again today and no one has invited me to hang out."	Weren't your friends from English class out sick the last couple of days? Maybe some of my peers are as introverted as I am, and I may need to initiate contact with them. This is probably not about me; I'm feeling lonely, but I am not alone. How can I be gentler with myself? How can I foster new relationships with my peers in and out of school?
"I'll never try out for the soccer team. I won't make it anyway."		

Thought	Trigger (Event or Situation)	Alternative Explanations
"I can't show up to that party, Mom. If I go, people will know how awkward I am and will laugh at me."		

Step #3: Reframe the Situation

Fear creates deep inaccuracies and skews our thinking in ways that cause more anxiety, not less. Many of us overestimate the likelihood that our fears will actually occur. These strategies will help you pause and think about your world more accurately. When you reframe your situation in a positive way, you are able to see possibilities you weren't aware of before.

Here's how to do it:

Steps to Reframing the Situation

- **View your situation more positively.** Is there something you will get to do because things didn't work out the way you thought they should?

- **Identify benefits.** Find the benefits in the situation you face.

- **Find what you can change.** If you could, what parts of your situation would you most like to change?

- **Discover the humor.** Find the aspects of your situation that are so absurd that you can't help but laugh.

Write these out at first, do it with someone, and then over time, you'll be able to do it in your head.

When you notice the ANTs coming out to play—when a thought comes into your head that you're not quite sure what to do with but you suspect it doesn't belong—there is another strategy for stamping them out. It's an acronym that can help you determine whether it's a thought worth smashing and getting rid of or one worth holding on to: THINK.

How to THINK

T — Is It True? A brain in stress or anxiety is extremely compelling. It convinces us that all of the hardships in life (difficult break-ups, global warming, not getting accepted to the college we wanted) were the result of our poor choices. It can convince us that we "can never get anything right." When this pops up, refute the lies with truths.

H — Is It Helpful? Stress and overthinking are common symptoms of an anxious or depressed brain. Something small and insignificant can keep us up half the night falsely assuming, "If I think about it a lot, a solution will come." Overthinking a problem rarely generates a solution; instead, it elevates anxiety. According to one study, 85 percent of what we worry about never occurs![39]

I — Is It Inspiring? The negative inner critic is less than inspiring or uplifting. It loves to speak in absolutes. Critical statements such as, "I will never get anything right," and "I will always be a failure" are the mainstays of stress and anxiety. When you hear these rigid statements, seek out the exception and use others as an example. So, eliminate the words: "always" and "never." They are not inspiring, and they certainly are not true.

N — Is It Necessary? Given the large number of thoughts our brain generates in a day, much of what we think about is negative and repetitive. Because the mind tends to focus on unfounded fears and worries, it is important to take a step back and evaluate the thoughts that arise. With every self-critical thought, pause and ask yourself if it is necessary.

K — Is It Kind? Self-compassion involves speaking to yourself kindly as you would to a dear friend who is suffering. When experiencing stress or high anxiety, we often struggle with self-compassion because the lies make us believe we are unworthy of kindness or care. Self-compassion may be the last thing you feel like having, but it really does help. Think about what you might say to a close friend or a small child in the same situation. Replacing self-criticism with self-compassion will lead to more acceptance over time.

So, when you think a thought, don't forget to THINK about what kind of thought you are allowing to take control of you. You don't always have control of your situation and the things happening around you, or even the emotions that flare up as a response to them. But you *do* have the ability to control what kind of thoughts you allow to take hold of you and cause you to keep spiraling downward in your anxiety. **When you make it a habit to challenge your thoughts, you can break the spiral of negative thinking.**

Here are some other ways to increase positive thoughts or neutralize the negative ones:

Smile.
(Acting calm, happy, or confident can cause you to feel those things, even if you don't.)

List **three things** you are grateful for each day.

Do something for **someone else.**

Use **positive** quote cards or affirmations each morning.

If you catch a negative self-talk moment, **ask yourself,** "Would I say this to a friend?" If the answer is "No," then you know it's not helpful to say to yourself.

Memorize and recite **Scripture.**

Remind yourself that you are **good enough.**

Clean or declutter something.

Watch a **funny** movie.

HOW CAN I INVITE GOD IN? READ THE BIBLE

Remember the saying, "An idle mind is the devil's workshop"? With that in mind, how then do you safeguard your mind? When the enemy attacks, he usually starts with our minds. The reason for that is that it's an easy entry point. Our actions first begin to take root with thoughts that pop up in our minds. How do you close down the entry points that allow lies to creep into your thoughts?

Fill your mind with truth. The Bible is full of truth. When you read the Bible on a regular basis, you are helping your mind reframe back to God's truth.

The Bible is a source of truth that helps to close down the pathways of lies and allow you to . . .

- Make every thought captive and obedient to Christ. (See 2 Corinthians 10:4-5.)

- Believe what He says about you.

- Trust in His promises.

When anxiety shows up, trying to trick you with lies and convince you to live in fear, pick up the Bible or look up some verses on the YouVersion app. You will find a plethora of wisdom, comfort, and everlasting hope. Your entire perspective on life will begin to shift as you dwell on the true words of God.

Remember the THINK acronym? Here is the Bible's version:

"Finally, brothers and sisters, whatever is true, whatever is noble, whatever is right, whatever is pure, whatever is lovely, whatever is admirable—if anything is excellent or praiseworthy—THINK about such things" (Philippians 4:8, NIV, emphasis ours).

God's words are true. And He gives us a way to center our minds around truth.

"Every word of God proves true; he is a shield to all who come to him for protection" (Proverbs 30:5, NLT).

Journaling what you read in the Bible is a great way to think deeper about the truth you are reading. This spiritual tool will help you reframe anxiety and remember what's true about God and what God says about you. You can use prompts like these:

1. What is one verse I read today?

_____

2. What is happening around this verse? Who is speaking? Where did this story take place?

_____

_____

_____

3. How can this apply to my life today?

_____

_____

_____

Write some of your favorite verses on a card or Post-it® note and place them where you can see them. Even better, memorize them. Then you will be able to fill your mind and heart with instant truth from God's Word that will help you reframe your mind in the moments you need it most.

Recap

Anxious thoughts lead us to feel like we are spiraling out of control. But the reality is you have control over the thoughts that you allow to take hold of you. You can get rid of those pesky negative thoughts by recognizing your thinking traps, identifying your triggers and worries, and finally reframing them to reflect a more accurate representation of reality. When you think a thought, THINK about whether it is true, helpful, inspiring, necessary, or kind. This is not always easy to do, so invite God to help you take every thought captive by reading the Bible and discovering what is true about God and what He is able to do, and what He says is true about you.

THE LIE
I have no control.

THE TRUTH
I can control my thoughts.

WHAT CAN I DO?
Reframe negative thoughts.

HOW CAN I INVITE GOD IN?
Read the Bible.

SIX

THE LIE:
I'M GOING TO MISS OUT

"I have struggled with anxiety since I was a kid. I had one of my first anxiety attacks when I went on a trip with some friends, away from home. I didn't really like being home, though. I tried to hang out with my friends as much as I could. My home life was really tense, and I always felt the need to be the peacekeeper. Sometimes, I would just hide in the bathroom or spend hours on my phone just to escape the pressure of trying to always make things right. When I tried to talk about my anxiety with my parents, they blew it off. I love my parents, they are great people, but my dad always had a fix like, "Well, that's not real" or, "Just focus more on school." And my mom just tried to pray my anxiety away. So instead of staying home where I felt anxious all the time, I tried to stay busy enough so that I wouldn't think about my anxiety. But it followed me.

Learning more about anxiety from reading and talking with a counselor helped me realize that I am not just "crazy." I also realized that being busy all the time doesn't help. In fact, it just makes it worse."

—Emery, College Senior, 21

Have you ever felt "phone-liness"?

Urban Dictionary defines *phone-liness* as the uncomfortable urge to look at your phone when left alone at a dinner table, waiting in line, or any other public place.

I know, *none* of you who are reading this have *ever* been guilty of that. But some of us are! Some days, I (Will) can't even sit through a red light without grabbing my phone and opening an app.

Want to hear something absolutely *terrifying*?

Research shows that the average person touches their phone 2,600 times per day![40] Yes, you read that right. Two thousand six hundred times. For some of you, that might be more, or it might be way less.

The point is you and I are living in an age of digital addiction. If we're being honest, we probably all fall somewhere on the spectrum of being addicted to technology.

If we're not careful, our fear of missing out will make digital addiction that much worse. We don't want to miss out on the latest trend or be the only person at the table who doesn't understand the joke.

This fear of missing out can make us want to be connected to our devices at all times. But here's the reality: We can consume all the content in the world but never actually feel full.

Like when you're hungry and you snack on potato chips. You could probably eat a whole bag of chips but not feel like your hunger is satisfied.

Why?

The simplest answer is we are living in a digital world where God created us for face-to-face connection.

Research shows that our brains don't respond to digital connection the same as it does when we're face to face. In fact, on social media, there can be this disconnect where we are "interacting" with others but not actually seeing their faces or hearing their voices.

This disconnect is why people, in general, tend to be meaner on social media (in comments, for instance) than they might be face to face. Because when you're face to face with someone, you see their facial expressions, you hear their tone of voice, and you see their non-verbals.

I Have So Many Friends, But I Feel So Lonely

This feeling of disconnection leads us to another painful reality that social media eagerly highlights for us. As we mindlessly scroll through our feeds, we are made aware of all the things we are missing out on that everyone else is doing, who they are hanging out with, and when we're not invited. And so not only do we feel phone-ly, we actually really do feel lonely. What would have been a quiet evening enjoying time with family or doing something fun on our own is sabotaged by hurt feelings and knowing we've been left out of something we all feel drawn to, a sense of real community, face to face, with real people.

Social rejection is a terrible feeling, and chances are, your emotional memory hasn't forgotten the moments you have felt left out and alone.

When we see friends hanging out without us, our minds instantly go to the worst-case scenario. We may start to believe lies like, "They must not like me," or "They didn't want me to come." When, in reality, there could be a hundred different reasons why you didn't get an invite. (See chapters 3 and 5 on how to deal with the emotions of feeling left out.)

Does Scrolling Fuel My Anxiety?

So you can see there are many reasons our addiction to technology and social media feeds can easily become the culprit that keeps us needlessly spiraling in our anxiety. Research shows that the more time you spend on your phone, the more negative your mood becomes. The most common negative moods are feelings of anxiety, loneliness, and sadness.[34]

I doubt any of us have a hard time believing this is true because we've all experienced it to some extent.

The amount and kind of information at our fingertips is mind-boggling. We are instantly aware of every tragedy, every social injustice, the latest trends and fashions, our friends' whereabouts, and how well we measure up to everyone else. We can't discount the many positives that this easy access to information allows us, but too much of it for too long can leave us feeling overwhelmed, burdened, left out, and ultimately anxious.

Not only that but when we are constantly on screens, we are *overstimulated*. You might think this is a good thing, but your central nervous system doesn't. When you're going from one thing to another, you overwhelm your senses, not to mention all the emotions you have to navigate.

Am I Doing Too Much?

Speaking of being overwhelmed, let's consider things other than technology. Maybe you don't have a problem with phone addiction. Even if you have healthy boundaries with technology, what does your social, academic, and extra-curricular life look like?

Are you the kind of person who wants to be a part of everything all the time, involved in every activity, participating in all the things because you don't want to miss out on something potentially important? There might be a slight chance you could miss an opportunity, feel out of the loop, or miss the boat!

If this is you, you probably have a hard time saying no to anything, so you overcommit, overpromise, do too much, and try to be all things to all people. In the end, you stress yourself out to the point you nose-dive into the anxiety spiral.

On a scale of one to ten, how would you rank your stress level based on overcommitments?

0   1   2   3   4   5   6   7   8   9   10

This might sound weird, but do you find yourself doing some of your best thinking or coming up with your best ideas when you're in the shower? Maybe it's because you finally have the brainwidth to actually do some thinking.

Why is that? Likely, the shower is one of the most consistent places where you don't have your phone or technology, and you have few or no distractions. So you actually give yourself a chance to breathe, process, think, and maybe even cry if you need to.

This brings us to the truth of this chapter.

THE TRUTH: I NEED A BREAK

It may sound counterintuitive, but when the world (or your brain) is telling you, "You're missing out," there's a good chance that what you truly need is a break.

This might mean a break from technology and your over-commitments.

Okay, you might be freaking out right now, no matter how old you are.

I know.

I KNOW.

Don't shoot the messenger.

It's not just teens and young adults who need a break. Adults do too. In fact, older adults can be worse sometimes. We all need to evaluate how well we do with this.

Why? Because God created all of our minds, bodies, and hearts the same way—with a need for rest and a need for true connection.

Remember the amygdala? Another way you can think of it is like a little alarm that goes off in your brain. When you don't have enough time between the different hard things you experience in life, you don't give your amygdala enough time to heal and get back to "normal."

Over time, this can lead to your amygdala being overactive, like a nosy neighbor who just doesn't know how to relax! This can breed feelings of anxiety (you always feel like something bad is about to happen), or even worse, panic attacks.

When life seems to be spinning out of control, the feeling of safety seems out of reach. Anxiety tells you danger is right around the corner, keeping you on edge and constantly aware and exhausted. That's why needing a break doesn't mean you're weak. It just means you're human.

The healing that we all need from the hard things we go through in life, big and small, can only happen when we slow down long enough to process them.

WHAT CAN I DO? REST

Remember, stress and anxiety are normal aspects of dealing with life, but so is rest. While you may not be able to avoid stressful situations in life, you need to be able to find rest even in the middle of difficult seasons.

There are many healthful ways to rest that don't necessarily include sleep. (We already mentioned prioritizing sleep in chapter 5.)

Here are a few ideas to get you started:

- Go for a walk
- Exercise
- Take a nap
- Do some stretching
- Take a shower
- Practice breathing exercises
- Meet a friend for coffee
- Spend some time journaling
- Listen to music
- Create a retreat

Actively resting helps us to reset. One thing that might help you develop the practice of rest is to have a designated area—somewhere inviting where you enjoy spending time that can also act as a reminder if you see it daily.

This could be as simple as creating a cozy corner in your bedroom. Or maybe it's a spot near your house where you like to spend time in nature. Maybe it's a nearby park. Maybe you find a quiet place to draw, paint, or play an instrument.

Even just being still and listening to instrumental music can help your mind and body have the time it needs to rest and reset.

We've created a playlist of some of our favorite relaxing music just for you.

One of the best ways you can rest from the chaos around you is to practice being present, instead of dwelling on something that has happened in the past or worrying about the future. This can help you rest and feel calm. But learning to do this takes practice.

How Do I Practice Being Present?

Research has shown a very effective way to practice being present is through mindfulness. Mindfulness is a mental state achieved by focusing your awareness on the present moment, while calmly and non-judgmentally acknowledging and accepting your feelings, thoughts, and bodily sensations. Yes, all of them. Even the uncomfortable ones. Don't worry, we'll show you how in a minute.

Mindfulness disrupts the underlying power of anxiety. New research indicates that mindfulness is just as effective as anxiety medication for some people.[35] Admittedly, it's not an easy practice initially, but it's super helpful and much simpler than you think. In my clinical practice, I (Dr. Chinwé) like to introduce mindfulness as a good remedy for the multitasking, hyper-digital, anxiety-producing world we live in. Mindfulness is a moment-by-moment decision to be present exactly where you are. Not in the past, not in the future. Right here. Right now.

Exercise #1: News Feed

Imagine a news feed across the bottom of a computer screen. There's a bit of news, then some white space, then more news, and so on. Your thoughts are like the news. There's always more! Now consider the white space between the thoughts. Close your eyes. Place your inner focus on the constant stream of thoughts scrolling across the TV of your mind. See the scrolling thoughts floating in space or across a TV screen, whatever image works for you.

Don't pay attention to the thoughts in detail. Let them scroll by; do not cling to them or reject them. Just notice them. Acknowledge each thought. Don't try to suppress it. Remember, it is just a thought; it is not real, and having it does not require you to act upon it.

Once you acknowledge the thought, it often disappears.

Exercise #2: Brain Dump

Doing a "core dump" of your mind can be helpful when you have a constant swirl of thoughts disrupting your sleep or just your peace. Here's how to do it:

1. Get in a quiet place where you will not be disturbed. Turn off phones and all devices. Have a piece of paper and pen ready.

2. Set the vibe. Maybe diffuse some essential oils, light a candle, or sit by a window.

3. Ask God to enter into your thoughts.

4. Set a timer for fifteen to twenty minutes.

5. Notice your breath. Is it quick and shallow, or slow and deep? Just notice.

6. Now start writing about any issue you are anxious about, want to clear from your mind, want to understand or be free from or have a question about. Just write— unedited and unpunctuated. When the sheet is full, if you need more room to write, turn it over, then upside down, on its side, and so forth to continue writing. You will not be reading this later, so there's no point in using more than one sheet of paper. The only purpose is to keep writing until the timer sounds.

7. When the time is up, either burn the paper or tear it up and throw it in the trash. Wash your hands and change your physiology (jump up and down for a moment or roll your shoulders, for example).

8. Now, try to get some rest.

Whenever you feel a non-positive emotion, use that as an opportunity to initiate a mindful pause. As you continue this practice, you may notice a decreased reaction to triggers. Your mind will learn to refrain from judging yourself (and others) and instead to simply be present, even during challenging times. This is a process that you can do independently, or it can be facilitated by a therapist, small group leader, or a friend.

Spiritual practices such as prayer and stillness are also forms of mindfulness that greatly and proactively buffer the effects of negative life events by acknowledging them (rather than avoiding them), which eventually restores hope.

Gratitude is also powerful in those moments. While praying or meditating, consider recalling recent positive experiences and think about those things you're grateful for.

Here's more guidance from Dr. Chinwé on how to practice being present.

What If I Don't Have Time to Rest?

Ironically, one of the barriers to getting rest is not setting any boundaries in your life. There are certain guardrails you can set for yourself to prevent needless stress and anxiety. When you are intentional ahead of time with the things you allow to capture your time and energy, you give yourself the margin you need for rest.

Setting boundaries can be tricky. Keeping them can be even trickier. Especially when you're not the one dictating your schedule or expectations.

To set personal boundaries, ask yourself: What kind of person do I want to be? What kind of life do I want to live? Do I want to live a life that is free of debilitating anxiety, or even the gnawing kind of anxiety? How important is it to me that I experience freedom and peace?

The boundaries you set for yourself will help set you up for the life you want to live. So whether it is the foods you choose to eat, the people you hang around, the information you consume, or the activities you decide to participate in, all of those correlate with the amount of stress (or anxiety) you invite into your life.

Sometimes you are at the mercy of someone else, like a boss, a coach, or a parent. You can't control how much homework a teacher or professor gives you. You can't control whether a friend, parent, or coach is asking too much. But sometimes the choice really is up to you.

When you advocate for boundaries and set them for yourself, you can eliminate many of the battles raging in your mind. Here are a few things to consider when you are setting the boundaries for a more carefree life—a life beyond the anxiety spiral.

1. **Learn to Say No**

   If you are anything like me (Will), then you have a "no" problem. For some reason, my lips and tongue have a hard time saying the word no. Actually, it transfers to my fingers too.

Text from my friends:

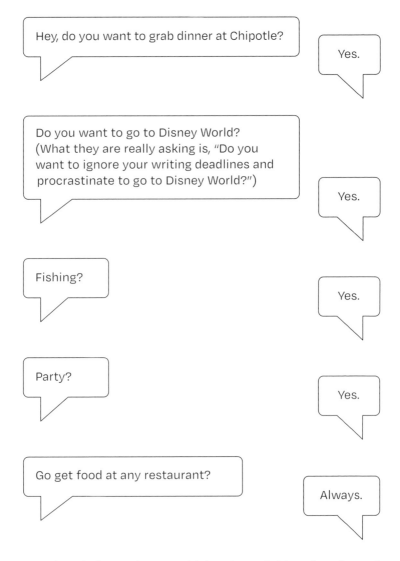

Hey, do you want to grab dinner at Chipotle?

Yes.

Do you want to go to Disney World?
(What they are really asking is, "Do you want to ignore your writing deadlines and procrastinate to go to Disney World?")

Yes.

Fishing?

Yes.

Party?

Yes.

Go get food at any restaurant?

Always.

I love being active. As a high extrovert, I love hanging out with my friends. So I tend to say yes, when I should really say no. Maybe you can relate. Maybe you, like me, tend to overcommit yourself to experiences and activities. While it can all seem fun and energizing to be constantly busy, eventually, it wears you down. I constantly have to remind myself that boundaries are needed, even for fun things, but also for some of the more serious and important things. You don't have to do or be a part of everything.

2. **Set Limits on Social Media**

One of the best ways to make room for rest is to create boundaries with technology. We weren't meant to be exposed to infinite amounts of disturbing news stories, political opinions, perfect images, and the full extent of what everyone is doing and thinking at all times. The amount of anxiety that builds from consuming that kind of information can be overpowering on its own. Here are some suggestions to consider:

▶ Carve out time each day when you put your phone away.
▶ Set time limits on certain apps
  or delete them altogether.
▶ Unfollow accounts that you know are not helpful.
▶ Give yourself a time limit on video games.
▶ Put your phone in another room before you go to bed.

It might be really hard to set some of those boundaries, especially at the beginning. If that's you, try starting with a small goal. Even just five minutes of putting your phone away. Then try working your way up to a bit more time.

Try this: For one week, try to decrease your information intake by just 5 percent. If your brain is processing too much information, a simple decrease can help create some space. Space for rest.

HOW CAN I INVITE GOD IN? BE STILL

Seventeenth-century scientist and theologian Blaise Pascal made this observation in his *Pensees* (section 139), "All the unhappiness of men arises from one single fact, that they cannot stay quietly in their own room."[44] The idea of being alone in silence is a scary notion to many. But with God, you're never alone. When you invite Him into your fears, worries, and anxiety, you can find rest.

Silence and solitude are lost spiritual disciplines in our modern-day world. We are moving incredibly fast as a culture. In the end, it leaves us feeling starved for rest. Our souls are desperate for quiet reflection in the presence of God. But here's what God asks us to do:

". . . Be still, and know that I am God" (Psalm 46:10, NIV).

This idea of silence and solitude is something Jesus modeled while He was on Earth.

"But Jesus often withdrew to lonely places and prayed" (Luke 5:16, NIV).

Jesus must have thought being alone in silence was important to His own well-being. It just so happens also to be a practice that is exceptionally beneficial for our mental health.

If you are like most people, the idea of sitting still in silence is a little unnerving. Sometimes we are afraid of stillness, allowing our emotions to play out, thinking that if we stepped all the way into our emotions and questions that we've ignored and avoided, we'd somehow be overtaken by them. We get it. But the truth is our emotions are normal, and the more we try to suppress our emotions and questions, the more power they have.

We talked earlier about the positive outcomes of practicing mindfulness. The cool thing about mindfulness—like prayer—is that it generates a natural feeling of relaxation. The reason why is that it is directly activating the part of the nervous system that speaks to the fight-or-flight response as if to say, "It's okay, just chill. Everything is under control."

When we invite God into this honest place of acknowledging and accepting our feelings and thoughts, something even more powerful takes place. We feel seen by God. There is a supernatural connection that takes place when we stop and honestly present ourselves to God and acknowledge that He is in control. He is God. God loves meeting people in this honest place because it's in the silence and solitude that we can truly pause to invite Him into our inner world.

We love the way Ruth Haley Barton explains this: "You are like a jar of river water all shaken up. What you need is to sit still long enough that the sediment can settle and the water can become clear."[45] Being still with God is a great way to allow the sediment of anxiety to settle so you can feel safe again.

How to Practice Mindful Silence and Solitude With God

1. **Find a space.**
   It's important to establish a space to stop and be present with God. You can create a corner in your room that feels comfortable or a chair in your house. Personally, I (Will) like to sit outside in my hammock.

2. **Choose a time.**
   Try to find time to practice stillness. Whether in the morning, afternoon, or nighttime, pick a time that works best for your schedule. Set a reminder on your phone or place a physical reminder somewhere you will see it. For instance, place your Bible on your pillow in the morning to remind yourself to do it at night before you go to bed.

3. **Set a duration.**

   Try to start with three minutes. Then increase the time gradually. Many people find ten minutes a day very helpful. The amount of time is not as important as simply doing it regularly.

4. **Get comfortable.**

   Set your feet on the floor or ground, sit in a comfortable position, and breathe deeply. Start with a simple prayer that expresses your desire to invite God to be with you. Keep it short, under ten words. As you practice being still with God, give yourself lots of grace. Your mind may wander, and you might get distracted, but gently refocus your mind back to being present with God. Let distractions come and let them float by like a leaf in a flowing river.

5. **Close your time with gratitude.**

   Close your time of stillness with gratitude. Thank God for rest and for His presence. Go ahead and write down 10 things you are grateful for today.

   _____   _____

   _____   _____

   _____   _____

   _____   _____

   _____   _____

As you continue to practice stillness, you can use this time to ask yourself questions to notice what is true about you. Questions that help you check in with yourself can help you be present.

- ▸ How have I been feeling lately?
- ▸ What's been consuming my thoughts?
- ▸ How do I feel emotionally?
- ▸ What does my soul need right now?

Recap

The fear of missing out or being left out leads us to believe that we have to overcommit, always say yes, and be constantly in the know about everything going on around us. This is a trap that leads us to exhaustion and needless anxiety. The truth is you need a break from the chaos. Rest is essential to our well-being. Practice being present and make room for rest by setting up boundaries in the areas of your life you are allowing to take control and feed your anxiety. Invite God into the chaos by resting in Him and learning to be still in His presence.

THE LIE
I am going to miss out.

THE TRUTH
I need a break.

WHAT CAN I DO?
Rest.

HOW CAN I INVITE GOD IN?
Be still.

SEVEN

THE LIE:
I CAN DO IT ALONE

"I choked. It was the day of the big game. I didn't realize how much my anxiety had worsened until I had a full-blown panic attack in the middle of a game, in front of everyone—the fans, my family, and my entire basketball team and coach. It had happened a couple of times before during practice. I thought about telling someone how I'd been feeling, but I didn't think anyone would understand. Or worse, I would be thought of as weak. But then it happened . . . right there . . . in a game . . . in the middle of half-court. The cat was clearly out of the bag. At that point, I wasn't sure what was worse, the panic attack—causing my chest to throb and my throat to close up—or the fact that all my classmates and teammates were watching. But to my surprise, once I was able to open up about what I was going through, my team rallied around me. I discovered I wasn't alone. My coach helped me tell my parents, who found a therapist for me. All of this eventually led me to see that there were so many people who cared about me."

—Josh, High School Senior, 17

If you relate to Josh's story, you're not alone. Sports performance anxiety, also known as competitive anxiety, is widespread. In fact, 30 to 60 percent of athletes have experienced it.[46]

Sources of sports-related anxiety include self-imposed pressure to master an athletic maneuver perfectly, worries caused by an overly aggressive coach or family member, or stress about letting down one's teammates. One of the things that intensifies performance anxiety the most is the evaluative component.

I don't know about you, but I (Dr. Chinwé) do not enjoy being constantly observed and evaluated. I'd feel like I was in a fishbowl! In sports, athletes are frequently under scrutiny by fans, coaches, and teammates. This level of scrutiny can lead to many difficult emotions (for example: embarrassment, loss of confidence, and even shame). And, for professional athletes, unresolved performance anxiety can ultimately impact their careers.

There are several well-known examples of famous athletes who experienced anxiety. From three of the greatest Olympians in modern times, swimmer Michael Phelps, gymnast Simone Biles, and skier Lindsey Vonn, to NBA all-stars Kevin Love and DeMar DeRozan, superstar athletes have publicly (and bravely) opened up about their own mental health battles in an effort to take away the stigma of anxiety.

Ninety percent of athletic performance is the result of mental processes. Anxiety and its associated physical symptoms (like hyperventilation, shortness of breath, a racing heart, and nausea) can interfere with athletic achievement, and even lead athletes to push pause or quit their sport.

Lindsey Vonn, a three-time Olympic gold medalist, once stated, "I wish I had been able to—or been strong enough—to talk about it back in the early parts of my career."[47] Vonn points to support from loved ones and mental health professionals for giving her the strength and courage to speak transparently about her mental health journey.

Sometimes anxiety surfaces after a tragic loss. Dallas Cowboys quarterback Dak Prescott faced anxiety and depression following his brother's suicide and their mother's cancer diagnosis and subsequent death.

In an interview, Prescott encouraged others to seek support, stating that those losses (compounded by isolation due to the pandemic) intensified his anxiety. "It creates new emotions— emotions that I've never felt before. I obviously got the help that I needed and was very open about it. I think that's why I was fortunate enough to get over it, as not all of us are."[48]

If you've read this far in the book (whether you're an athlete or not), you've probably been searching for help with how to manage your anxiety for a while. You may have tried a number of strategies, from pushing down your worries to distracting yourself, to suffering in silence. Whether you've begun to use the tools and strategies in this book or not, this section will help you determine how you can benefit from the support of a caring adult like a parent or small group leader, or even a skilled professional.

What Keeps Me Silent?

But before we get into all of the help that's available, let's first deal with what prevents us from reaching out for help. For many, it is simply a result of feeling shame.

Shame and Guilt

Shame and guilt are two closely related emotions, but shame is deeper and much more dangerous. Many of us can relate to times when we have felt embarrassed or guilty about something we did or said. For example, if you make a mistake, or say something awkward in class, or hurtful to a friend, that's when guilt comes into play. Guilt can keep us in line when we veer too far from our moral standards. Shame is different, and shame makes it personal. Essentially, guilt says, "I did something bad," whereas shame says, "I am bad." Shame isn't just about what happened but how we *feel* about ourselves in relation to what happened.

Shame is biologically stressful, producing elevated cortisol (stress hormones) levels in our body.[49] Shame is also linked to poor recovery outcomes in almost every mental health condition: depression, addiction, trauma, and eating disorders, to name a few.

Sadly, shame is also a barrier to getting help for one's anxiety.

Several researchers suggest that high levels of shame, also known as toxic shame, are also associated with early childhood abuse or neglect. Toxic shame makes you feel worthless. This type of shame surfaces when you are treated poorly by others, but then you internalize that treatment into a negative belief about yourself. We tend to be most vulnerable to this type of treatment and the development of this belief system during childhood or adolescence.

Researchers discovered that experiencing chronic shame as a child can actually change your neurobiology, making you more prone to negative thinking (think more ANTs) and isolation. These unwanted feelings of shame can lead to deep feelings of unworthiness and inadequacy.[50]

They can also keep people from getting the help they need.

Here's the thing: People who feel unworthy or inadequate rarely ask for help. They often wrongly think they don't deserve help or blame themselves for whatever they're going through.

Stigma

Along with shame, another reason some individuals don't seek help for their anxiety, or frankly, any mental health problem, is stigma. While conversations about mental health are being discussed more widely, there still remains a stigma when it comes to seeking help for mental health challenges in many cultures, specifically communities of color. According to research, the reasons many people of color cite for the stigma include:

- **Lack of understanding**. Not understanding about mental health issues can lead to denial or neglect of worsening mental health problems. This is seen especially among first-generation AAPI (Asian American/Pacific Islander) immigrants.

- **Feelings of shame.** People can feel shame for even considering they might have a mental health challenge.

- **Fear.** Sometimes people are afraid others will find out. They fear the negative opinions and judgments that will come.

- **Being judged as weak.** Having a mental health challenge has been considered a weakness. Some members of African-American, Black, Asian-American, Pacific Islander, and Hispanic or Latin communities believe it is a source of shame, not just to themselves, but also to their families or entire culture.[51]

You may relate to one or more of these stigmas, even if you don't identify as a member of a community of color. The desire to "save face," "keep up a facade," or "protect" the family's name can often discourage individuals from seeking help until there is a crisis. If you are struggling with anxiety or anything else, please know this: Suffering in silence is neither noble nor necessary. The truth is, it's okay to ask for and receive help.

THE TRUTH: IT'S OKAY TO ASK FOR HELP

By now, I (Dr. Chinwé) hope we've established that managing your anxiety doesn't always happen all by yourself—it often happens with the help of others. I teach my clients that while they won't be able to control all of life's obstacles, such as the pressure that comes from being an elite athlete, or the stress that comes from just being a human, they can control how they respond. And while there are and will be barriers, we hope you will see the importance of facing—and not avoiding—those barriers. But we're not going to lie. It's not always an easy road. Managing anxiety, especially the panic-attack variety, requires some heavy lifting. The good news is that you don't have to lift the heavy weight alone.

Have you ever heard the phrase "They are a self-made person"? It's an expression that means a person achieved success on their own. Nobody helped them.

There is no such thing as success without others. Think about it. Someone fed the "self-made person" as a baby. Someone taught them in elementary school. Someone coached them in middle school. Someone gave them a job in high school. Someone loaned them money. Someone gave them a shoulder to cry on. Someone, somewhere, somehow helped every success story.

Whether that story is an athletic, an academic, or a business success story, someone helped.

That is true when it comes to beating anxiety too. It's okay to ask for help. In fact, we need it.

Remember when we talked about how our brains are made of two parts? (See Chapter 2.) The logical left side and the emotional right side. When you experience stress, cortisol, a stress hormone, goes to work and can flood the brain. This causes a disconnection between the two sides. This is why when you feel really overwhelmed or highly stressed, it is often difficult to identify how you are feeling. But talking to someone who sees you and really listens helps re-engage the left side of the brain so you can logically process your thoughts and feelings. Connection with people actually helps reconnect what is disconnected in the brain. Oxytocin, another natural hormone, is released when we feel love and empathy from others. This hormone helps us feel safe and loved when anxiety is high.

Simply talking to someone about how you are feeling can decrease anxious feelings and help you focus on what is true instead of the lies of anxiety.

To put it another way, **talking to someone is 50 percent of the work in overcoming anxiety.**

It's that powerful.

WHAT CAN I DO? TALK TO SOMEONE

Who Do I Talk To?

Step 1: Consider the people you trust.

For most of you reading this book, we recommend you talk to your parents. For some of you, that may not be an option. In some instances, your parents may not be a safe place. In that case, we encourage you to talk to a trusted adult in your life. This could be a relative, a coach, a pastor, or a small group leader.

Step 2: Write down what you want to say.

This way, if you get nervous in the moment, you have something you can reference. It doesn't have to be long. It can be just a few words, like:

- ▸ Lately, I've been worrying a lot.
- ▸ I don't feel like myself, and I don't know why.
- ▸ I have felt uneasy lately.
- ▸ Sharing specific examples may be helpful as well.

Step 3: Ask them if you can set a time to talk.

We're not saying you can't just randomly bring it up after dinner. But if you want to make sure you have their full attention, sometimes it's helpful to ask your parents or the trusted adult in advance if you can set a time. This helps them know that it's something important and that they need to show up for you distraction-free.

Step 4: Just do it.

It doesn't have to be perfect. It doesn't have to be polished. It just has to be real. Share your heart, and ask them if they can help you. How they help you might depend on the extent that you are struggling.

- Mild symptoms → They can help you implement some of the practices we've discussed in this book, such as breathing, journaling, and stillness.

- Moderate symptoms → They can help you find a therapist in addition to practicing some of the skills in this book.

- Serious symptoms → They can intervene to make sure that you are safe and that you get the help that you need.

How Do I Find a Therapist?

Once you've tried different ways to manage your anxiety—including talking to someone—but your anxiety isn't improving or perhaps is getting worse, finding a skilled therapist is the next step. But where do you even start?

First, let's just acknowledge how scary that might feel to you. While getting help from a professional might be the right next step, it's very normal to feel hesitant. Even if you recognize you need support, the thought of talking to a complete stranger about your mental health may cause you anxiety by itself!

Going to counseling can certainly feel uncomfortable. But please know that it can be a very helpful choice. Take some time to do some light research about who might be a good fit for you.

While there are many therapies that will help you improve your anxiety-related symptoms, the most researched and the one that has proven to be the most effective in treating adolescent anxiety and depression is CBT or cognitive behavior therapy. (These are strategies we've also discussed in this book.)

If you aren't sure how to find a therapist, start by speaking to any professional you know in the medical or mental health community. In your school building, that might be a school nurse or your school counselor. You can even speak to a friend or a family member who has experienced anxiety and sought help. You can learn a lot from their positive and not-so-positive experiences.

People or organizations that can provide referrals:

- ‣ Pediatrician or family doctor
- ‣ Family friends
- ‣ Mental health professionals
- ‣ Youth pastors
- ‣ Small group leaders

For specific organizations, go to beyondthespiralbook.com.

How Do I Know If I Need Anxiety Medication?

Learning ways to manage your anxiety is hard work! If you have tried many of the tools we've mentioned in the book, like getting enough sleep and paying attention to your nutritional and exercise habits, but you are still not satisfied with your progress, this section is for you.

First, it's not your fault. As we've mentioned, anxiety is rampant among people of all ages right now. It's also genetic. Not to blame your parents or grandparents, but just saying. Sometimes you can do *all the things* and still need a bit more support.

Let us begin this section by clearly stating: Will and I are not medical doctors. Your pediatrician or psychiatrist is the best professional to advise you on whether—and when—to consider medication for anxiety. Unlike us, your doctor knows your full medical history, family health history, all the medications you've taken, and your current and various life stressors. So, if you are wondering whether anti-anxiety medication is right for you, please start there. However, in my role as a psychotherapist, I work very closely with many doctors who prescribe anti-anxiety medications to several of my clients. So I will share some general knowledge with the hope that it will give you some important information to consider as you and your family prepare to have the "medication conversation" with a medical professional.

Signs You Might Need Anxiety Medication

Anxiety feels horrible. It's in your head. It's in your body. It gets in the way. It will often be uncomfortable, but when it becomes your constant companion, it can feel debilitating. **Here are nine signs that may indicate that anxiety is getting in the way too much.**

1. You feel constantly on edge almost every day.

2. You feel irritable and on the brink of exploding on someone nearly every day.

3. Your thoughts are scattered, and no matter how hard you try, you can't concentrate on school or work.

4. You avoid things, even things that you enjoy or are good for you.

5. You've been in talk therapy for a month, and it isn't helping you to reduce your anxiety.

6. You toss and turn nearly every night. You just can't turn your brain off.

7. You have a stomachache that just doesn't go away.

8. You miss your friends and the old you. But you can't seem to make things better.

9. You're starting to feel sad and hopeless about things ever getting better.

If you experience most of these symptoms nearly every day, for close to six months, and it is interfering with most areas of your life, it might be time to speak to a mental health care provider about medication for anxiety.

How Do I Manage My Shame?

As we mentioned, the greatest barrier for some in getting help is feeling shame and that they don't deserve help. But don't let shame hold you back from experiencing freedom from your anxiety. Instead . . .

- **Recognize shame for what it is.** Recognizing when shame is affecting your thought life is crucial. Mindful awareness can alert you that shame may be surfacing in the form of unhelpful, unkind thoughts: "Why did I say that to him? I'm so stupid." "No one will ever understand how I feel." "I'm alone in this. Alone and unlovable."

- **Use the THINK acronym to determine if this thought is true, helpful, inspiring, necessary, or kind.** If it's not kind, it could be shame-filled and harmful if left unchecked for too long. We all make mistakes. Begin to disrupt the shame cycle by reminding yourself that mistakes will happen and are not a reflection of your worth. Learning to see mistakes as behaviors and not as a reflection of self-worth is essential to break the shame cycle that can perpetuate anxiety and depression.

- **Practice self-compassion.** Speak to yourself the way you would a friend who is hurting. Define yourself as a person worthy of love and compassion. Call out your God-given gifts and talents. Affirmations can help with this. Choose to be around others who do the same. If you were neglected or invalidated as a child, this might be hard for you at first. Through counseling, you can uncover the root causes of early childhood shame and begin to unravel some of the negative messages that have taken root.

- **Connect with friends or family.** Shame thrives in darkness, so keep shining your light on it by calling it out. Don't just keep it in your head—that's way too dark and exactly what shame wants! Find a friend who can provide an outlet for you to talk things out when needed. Shame also likes to isolate. Reconnecting with family, friends, and those who love you is essential to reducing feelings of shame. With the support of trusted friends, family members, and small group members, you can begin to see yourself as loved, valued, and worthy.

HOW CAN I INVITE GOD IN? CONNECT WITH OTHERS

We are created to need community. God made us in a way that connection is a key to life. It is a place of strength and a way to reduce anxiety. When we face stress or anxiety, our need for attachment goes up. This is natural. We are wired to need others in a safe community.

Belonging to God's family is a tool you can use to partner with God to break the anxiety loop. This could be as simple as going to church and finding a group of people you connect with and who can encourage you in your faith.

There is a lot in the Bible about the importance of community.

> "And let us consider how we may spur one another on toward love and good deeds, not giving up meeting together, as some are in the habit of doing, but encouraging one another—and all the more as you see the Day approaching" (Hebrews 10:24-25, NIV).

In his book *The Purpose Driven Life,* Rick Warren writes that we are "formed for God's family." That means God doesn't want you to just believe in Him; God wants you to belong to His family.[42] This is what church is all about—God's people coming together to worship, learn, and connect together. Since Jesus walked the earth, the Church (His followers) consistently came together for two reasons:

1. **The ministry of the Word.** This is where His followers listen to someone teach the truth from God's Word.

2. **The ministry of the table.** This is the tradition of God's people coming together relationally. Usually, this meant eating together and connecting. If you've ever been to a church

picnic, a sports banquet, a wedding reception, or an event with food trucks, that is an example of the ministry of the table. Jesus sat at a lot of tables. His first miracle was while He was sitting at a wedding reception table. He infamously sat at tables and ate with "sinners and tax collectors." He ate with Pharisees, and He ate with His disciples on the night one of them betrayed Him. Jesus sat at a lot of tables.

If you had a table that represented your key connections, what trusted person would sit at your table?

- ▸ Family member?
- ▸ Mentor?
- ▸ Pastor?
- ▸ Therapist?
- ▸ Friend?
- ▸ Coach?
- ▸ Teacher?
- ▸ Small group leader?

Whoever you choose, make sure they are people who lead you closer to God, share truth with you, encourage you, and help you to follow Jesus.

If your church has small groups, join a small group. Small groups are a great way to get connected with others in God's family, and oftentimes small groups are safe places to share about things that make you anxious. Remember, just talking about it is a big part of breaking the anxiety loop. And when you have others around you who are listening and encouraging you, it's even more powerful.

But don't feel like you need to share the deep stuff with everyone. **Go deeper and deeper with fewer and fewer.**

Anxiety loses power in the context of community because connection creates hope. When we feel love and empathy from others, it influences our brains toward hope. God wired us in this way. Just simply sharing with someone who we trust begins to increase our hope for the future. We find strength in connection, and the future doesn't feel as lonely.

What does your circle look like?

1. Write the names of people you already have in your circle.

2. Brainstorm a few other names you would like to include.

3. Make a plan to invite those people to be a part of your circle.

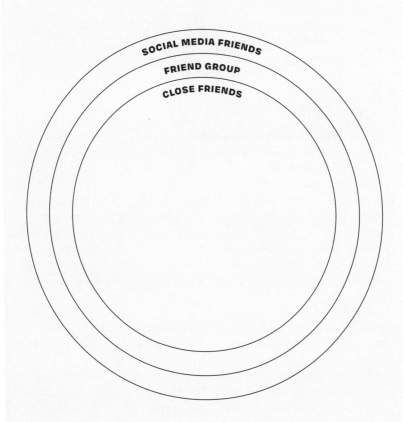

Recap

The lie that we should be able to get through our anxiety alone stems from the belief that we don't need to be a burden on anyone else, or maybe there's something wrong with us and we don't want others to know. But the truth is it's okay to ask for help. In fact, people want to help. We just need to take the next courageous step and talk to someone we trust, seek out a therapist if necessary, and look into medication when it becomes unmanageable. One of the best ways to get help is by going to church and connecting with God's family, where you will find good teaching, community, and encouragement.

THE LIE
I can do this alone.

THE TRUTH
It's okay to ask for help.

WHAT CAN I DO?
Talk to someone.

HOW CAN I INVITE GOD IN?
Connect with others.

EIGHT

YOU ARE NOT YOUR ANXIETY

That line might be the most relevant truth in the entire book. That truth is powerful because it combats every lie that anxiety tells you. Why?

Because what you allow to *define* you will ultimately *direct* you. Think about it. If you grow up in a family of die-hard fans of a specific football team, you will probably be a fan of that team too. You'll act like the other fans. You'll do the chomp, chop, chant, cheer, or wear the colors. You'll even identify with the mascot and say, "I am a (Tiger, Bulldog, Gator, Ray, Pirate, sparkle-colored fowl)."

The problem with mental health challenges like anxiety is that we can over-attach to the label of "having anxiety." **By over-attaching to a challenge, we start to believe the story the label tells us**. For instance, let's say you go through a tough season of life where some things happen that really stress you out. Maybe you start to experience situational anxiety. Perhaps you even experience a panic attack. Given the situation(s), your anxiety is expected and normal for your history and personality. But let's say you take steps to manage that anxiety. You start applying the tools in this book and even begin seeing a therapist or counselor. It's likely you will overcome the anxiety spiral.

Think of it this way.

If certain levels of anxiety are normal, and you are able to move your anxiety levels to managed levels, then do you still "have anxiety"? Sure. But we all do.

This matters because we can start believing the stories we tell ourselves and discredit our own growth. Or we start to believe a mental health challenge is our identity.

Maybe it would be more truthful to say, "I am prone to anxiety" or "I've experienced some challenges with anxiety." Because who you are is so much more.

The feeling of anxiety isn't a mental health challenge; it's human. It's part of how you're wired and how you adapt to life. However, as we've discussed throughout this book, anxiety can increase to a point where it becomes difficult to manage. With that challenge comes a wave of lies. Lies that, if we believe them, will reinforce our anxiety and cause us to spiral. **Anxiety likes to tell you, "There is something wrong with you." But actually, there is so much more that is right with you.**

Your mental health challenges do not define you.

Anxiety is a condition, not an identity. Depression is a diagnosis, not an identity.

You are not your anxiety.

For those of you who have faith in God, your identity is a child of God. You were created on purpose by God—made in God's image and knitted together in your mother's womb.

The good news is you don't have to choose between the two.

You can be a child of God who struggles with anxiety. And contrary to what you may have heard, you can be a Christian who struggles with depression.

After all, God didn't make us souls that are floating around without bodies. He also didn't make us bodies that are walking around without souls. He made us body, mind, AND spirit.

That said, when we are talking about anxiety, we would be wrong to ignore the physical, but we'd be equally wrong to ignore the spiritual.

In 2008, my (Will's) wife went through the hardest year of her life. Her parents split up, her 21-year-old cousin suddenly passed away, her grandfather completed suicide, and she was also by my side through the loss of my grandfather.

Through it all, many people told her, "Wow, you've been so strong through all of this." In response, she would say something to the effect of, "It's all because of God."

She genuinely meant it when she said it. And she genuinely thought that she was doing okay. Until one night when she woke up, gasping for air, hands on her chest. She ran out into the hallway and curled up in a fetal position, feeling like she was dying.

She and I were newly married, so I was terrified and had no idea what was happening. By the time I got my phone to call 911, she had realized she could still breathe, but continued experiencing an intense feeling that something was not okay. Adrenaline was rushing through her body, her muscles were tight, and she felt like she couldn't get a deep breath.

This was her first panic attack.

What followed was hours of feeling jittery, uneasy, short of breath, and, ultimately, more panic attacks. It became almost a nightly occurrence. She began to dread nighttime. She saw a doctor friend of ours because we didn't know what else to do. He prescribed an anxiety medication but told her to get into therapy.

Unfortunately, Arianne had grown up in a culture where therapy was fairly taboo. It was something people did only if they were on the verge of divorce or suicide. So she was resistant to the idea of going to counseling. She genuinely didn't think she needed it. In some way, she believed herself to be spiritual enough that counseling was not necessary.

Through loving encouragement from her mom and me, she finally started seeing a counselor, and she learned more about how complex the body and the mind are. She learned that in order to survive that year, she had stuffed down many of her emotions and not yet processed them. She learned that her body was still feeling unsafe after so much trauma in one year, hence the panic attacks in the middle of the night.

Outside of counseling, she would also spend intentional time in prayer and journaling. Through this process, she realized there was one underlying question that she needed to wrestle with:

Do I trust God with my life?

Do I trust God even though my parents split up?

Do I trust God even though my grandfather completed suicide?

Do I trust God even though life feels so fragile after all the death that I've seen this year?

Do I trust Him?

This isn't really a one-and-done kind of question. It's a question that as humans, we may wrestle with many times throughout our lives.

But here's the good news. No matter what changes about our lives . . .

God's goodness is unchanging.

And our identity as God's children is constant.

There will be times when you don't understand why something did or didn't happen. But **you can trust God with your entire life.**

You can trust Him because He is unchanging. Though much may change in our world, you can trust that God will never change His love, care, and compassion for you.

Not only can you trust God, but you can also trust what God says about you. When you allow that truth to define who you are, it will direct you. You can find strength in knowing you are more than your anxiety.

That truth is the most powerful truth you have to counter the lies of anxiety.

You are not your anxiety because God says you . . .

are God's child (John 1:12).
belong to God (1 Corinthians 6:20).
are forgiven (Ephesians 1:7; Colossians 1:14).
have purpose (Ephesians 2:10).
have hope (Ephesians 1:12).
are included (Ephesians 1:13).
are alive with Christ (Ephesians 2:5).
have peace (Ephesians 2:14).
are loved deeply (Ephesians 3:18).
have been called (Ephesians 4:1; 2 Timothy 1:9).
are dead to sin (Romans 6:2).
are not alone (Hebrews 13:5).
are victorious (1 John 5:4).
are set free (Romans 8:2; John 8:32).
are more than a conqueror (Romans 8:37).
are fearfully and wonderfully made (Psalm 139:14).

Your Creator knows the truth about you. You are *so much more* than your anxiety.

When you start paying attention to how God created your mind, spirit, and body, you will realize you have more control over anxiety than you think you do. Anxiety might continue to tell you lies and exaggerate your fears, but now you have the upper hand and the tools to help you manage your anxiety.

So continue trusting God with your everyday worries and future uncertainties, and make sure you don't listen to everything anxiety tells you. Then you will keep moving beyond the spiral—one day, one moment, and one deep breath at a time.

When Anxiety Tells You	Remember	Do This
I'm not safe.	I won't always feel this way.	Breathe.
I should just ignore it.	My emotions matter.	Feel emotions.
It's all in my head.	My mind is connected to my body.	Build healthy habits.
I have no control.	I can change my thoughts.	Reframe negative thoughts.
I'm going to miss out.	I need a break.	Rest.
I can do it all alone.	It's okay to ask for help.	Talk to someone.

ACKNOWLEDGMENTS

From Will:

While Chinwé and I are the authors of this book, the reality is a project like this is only possible because of hundreds of committed people. From students who shared their stories with us to editors and readers to family members that encouraged us. It took a team to write this book.

I want to thank my family. My wife Arianne for cheering me on, helping me with words when I got stuck and encouraging me to never give up. My kids, Liam, Reese, and Kinsley: I love being your Dad. You have taught me so much.

My friend Malike: Thank you for your voice and friendship. Also, thanks for always teaching me a new slang word. Lol.

Friends who pre-read and offered feedback: Crystal Chiang, Sarah Anderson, Shane Sanchez, Madi Jae Gosch, Lauren Sellers, Kevin Monahan, Kevin Norwood, Mike Ash, Kyle Jackson, Chad Moore, and too many others to name.

Teenagers who shared their stories with me at Youth Church in Fort Myers, Owasso First Assembly, and Grace Church Cape Coral. Thank you, Dusty Zarick, Taylor Brown, and Sam McDowell for sharing your wisdom on Gen Z.

I am most of all thankful for God's love, grace, and guidance through Jesus. I commit this work to Him, in gratitude for what He has done in my life. "Commit to the Lord whatever you do, and he will establish your plans" (Proverbs 16:3 NIV).

From Dr. Chinwé:
At the risk of sounding annoyingly cliché, I could not have completed this project without my amazing husband Lonnie. Thanks for all of the encouragement and for holding the fort down so well. Speaking of the fort, I want to thank my deeply considerate, and beautiful children, Jailyn, Brayden, and Noah.

Thanks to my mom and dad for repeatedly telling me you're proud of me. Your support means the world.

Finally, I must gratefully acknowledge all of the teenagers and young adults who have shared their stories and invited me into their space of healing throughout my almost two decades of counseling (Yikes!). I cherish and honor that privilege, and I honor you.

In essence, this book celebrates the courage that I see in young people, who every day, navigate a world much, much different from the one I grew up in.

Thank you for your bravery. And thank you for your willingness to grow.

From Both:
Thank you to the Parent Cue and Orange Publishing team for your commitment to helping the next generation and your commitment to this work. Special thanks to our editor Karen Wilson. Karen, you kept us on task and moving forward . . . THANK YOU.

To the Orange and PC Leadership Reggie Joiner, Kristen Ivy, Hannah Crosby and Mike Jeffries: Thank you for championing this project.

To the marketing, design and operations team: Brian Sharp, Melanie Williams, Brandon Carter, Ashley Shugart and Elizabeth Hildreth: Thank you for your hard work and dedication.

Finally, thank you to YOU, the reader. You inspire us. We love you and we believe in you.

NOTES

Chapter One

1 *"Anxiety Disorders." National Institute of Mental Health (NIMH),* accessed September 17, 2022. https://www.nimh.nih.gov/health/topics/anxiety-disorders.

2 "Prevalence of Any Anxiety Disorder Among Adolescents." *National Institute of Mental Health (NIMH),* accessed January 29, 2023. https://www.nimh.nih.gov/health/statistics/any-anxiety-disorder#part_2578.

3 "Prevalence of Any Anxiety Disorder Among Adolescents." *National Institute of Mental Health (NIMH),* accessed January 29, 2023. https://www.nimh.nih.gov/health/statistics/any-anxiety-disorder#part_2578.

4 Disclaimer: This quiz is modified from The Perceived Stress Scale (PSS). The PSS is a classic stress assessment instrument. This tool helps us understand how different situations affect our feelings and our perceived stress. The scores on this self-assessment do not reflect any particular diagnosis or course of treatment. They are meant as a tool to help assess your level of stress or anxiety.

5 "15 Common Anxiety Triggers & How to Cope With Them." *Choosing Therapy.* Accessed October 13, 2022. https://www.choosingtherapy.com/anxiety-triggers/.

6 "How Brain Neurons Change Over Time From Life Experience." *Verywell Mind.* Accessed September 17, 2022. https://www.verywellmind.com/what-is-brain-plasticity-2794886.

7 "Current Views on Neuropladticity: What Is New and What Is Old? | Acta Neuro." Accessed September 17, 2022. https://actaneuropsychologica.com/resources/html/article/details?id=199544&language=en.

Chapter Two

8 "Prevalence of Any Anxiety Disorder Among Adolescents." *National Institute of Mental Health (NIMH),* accessed January 29, 2023. https://www.nimh.nih.gov/health/statistics/any-anxiety-disorder#part_2578.

9 Hutcherson, Will, and Williams, Chinwé. Seen: Healing Despair and Anxiety in Kids and Teens through the Power of Connection. Cumming, GA: Parent Cue, a division of The reThink Group, Inc., 2021.

10 Strong, James. Strong's Exhaustive Concordance of the Bible. Nashville, Tennessee: Thomas Nelson, 1979.

This is an estimate from researching the original Greek and Hebrew words and combinations together for an estimate on how many times fear not or do not fear, or do not be afraid are listed.

Chapter Three

11 Chapman, B. P., Fiscella, K., Kawachi, I., Duberstein, P., & Muennig, P. (2013). Emotion suppression and mortality risk over a 12-year follow-up. *Journal of psychosomatic*

research, 75(4), 381–385. https://doi.org/10.1016/j. jpsychores.2013.07.014

12 Goff, Sissy. *Raising Worry-Free Girls: Helping Your Daughter Feel Braver, Stronger, and Smarter in an Anxious World.* Bloomington, MN: Bethany House Publishers, 2019.

13 "Panic Attacks and Panic Disorder - Symptoms and Causes." Mayo Clinic. Mayo Foundation for Medical Education and Research, May 4, 2018.

14 According to prevalence rates issued by the National Institute of Mental Health, an estimated 3.2 million teens aged 12 to 17 in the United States had at least one major clinical depressive episode. The prevalence rate was higher among teen females (20%) compared to teen males (6.8%) and was highest among multi-racial teens.

15 "Mental Illness." National Institute of Mental Health. U.S. Department of Health and Human Services. Accessed February 9, 2023. https://www.nimh.nih.gov/health/statistics/mental-illness.

16 "Rage Definition & Meaning." Merriam-Webster. Accessed December 5, 2022. https://www.merriam-webster.com/dictionary/rage.

17 The Feelings Wheel was adapted and used with the permission of Parent Cue. You can download the original here: https://theparentcue.org/resources/feelings-wheel/

18 1 Kings 19:3

19 Matthew 26:36, Mark 14:32

20 2 Corinthians 12:7-9

Chapter Four

21 Jacka, F.N., O'Neil, A., Opie, R. *et al*. A randomized controlled trial of dietary improvement for adults with major depression (the 'SMILES' trial). BMC Med 15, 23 (2017). https://doi.org/10.1186/s12916-017-0791-y.

22 "9 Foods That Help Reduce Anxiety." Medical News Today. MediLexicon International. Accessed March 17, 2023. https://www.medicalnewstoday.com/articles/322652.

23 Benbrook, Charles. "New Evidence Confirms the Nutritional Superiority of Plant-Based ...," October 2008. https://www.researchgate.net/publication/266820943.

24 Thirty-eight percent of people report overeating or eating unhealthy foods due to stress. Half of those surveyed (49%) reported unhealthy stress or emotional eating weekly or more. (See footnote 25).

25 Yau, Y. H., & Potenza, M. N. (2013). Stress and Eating Behaviors. Minerva endocrinologica, 38(3), 255–267.

26 "How Much Sleep Do Teenagers Really Need?" HCF. Accessed January 20, 2023. https://www.hcf.com.au/health-agenda/work-life/family/teens-and-sleep-how-much.

27 Gan, Gabriela, Alvaro Guevara, Michael Marxen, Maike Neumann, Elisabeth Jünger, Andrea Kobiella, Eva Mennigen, et al. "Alcohol-Induced Impairment of Inhibitory Control Is Linked to Attenuated Brain Responses in Right Fronto-Temporal Cortex." *Biological Psychiatry* 76, no. 9 (2014): 698–707. https:/doi.org/10.1016/j.biopsych.2013.12.017.

28 Day, Ed, and Chris Daly. "Clinical Management of the Alcohol Withdrawal Syndrome." *Addiction* 117, no. 3 (2021): 804–14. https://doi.org/10.1111/add.15647.

29 Wickham, Shay-Ruby, Natasha A. Amarasekara, Adam Bartonicek, and Tamlin S. Conner. "The Big Three Health Behaviors and Mental Health and Well-Being among Young Adults: A Cross-Sectional Investigation of Sleep, Exercise, and Diet." Frontiers. Frontiers, November 5, 2020.https://www.frontiersin.org/articles/10.3389/fpsyg.2020.579205/full?layoutOptions=Zm9vdGVyPW9mZixzaWRlYmFyPW9mZg.

30 Nagoski, Emily, and Amelia Nagoski. *Burnout: The Secret to Unlocking the Stress Cycle.* New York: Ballantine Books, 2020.

31 Cunliffe, Emily. "Your Body Can Produce 'Hope Molecules'." Medium. Curious, March 6, 2023. https://medium.com/curious/your-bodycan- produce-hope-molecules-9b015ce088e1.

32 Zhu, Cuizhen, Yu Zhang, Ting Wang, Yezhe Lin, Jiakuai Yu, Qingrong Xia, Peng Zhu, and Dao-min Zhu. "Vitamin D Supplementation Improves Anxiety but Not Depression Symptoms in Patients with Vitamin D Deficiency." *Brain and Behavior* 10, no. 11 (2020). https://doi.org/10.1002/brb3.1760.

33 Han, Bin, Fu-Xiang Zhu, Hai-Feng Yu, Si Liu, and Jun-Liang Zhou. "Low Serum Levels of Vitamin D Are Associated with Anxiety in Children and Adolescents with Dialysis." *Scientific Reports* 8, no. 1 (2018). https://doi.org/10.1038/s41598-018-24451-7.

34 Namazi, Nazli, Mostafa Qorbani, Gita Shafiee, Mohammad Hossein Ahmadian, Mohammad Esmaeil Motlagh, Mehdi Ebrahimi, Hamid Asayesh, Roya Kelishadi, and Ramin Heshmat. "Association of Vitamin D Concentrations with Subjective Health Complaints in Children and Adolescents: The Caspian-V Study." *BMC Public Health* 21, no. 1 (2021). https://doi.org/10.1186/s12889-020-10020-z.

35 Clear, James. *Atomic Habits: Tiny Changes, Remarkable Results: An Easy and Proven Way to Build Good Habits and Break Bad Ones.* London: Cornerstone Press, 2022.

Chapter Five

36 Amen, Daniel G. *Change Your Brain, Change Your Body: Use Your Brain to Get the Body You Have Always Wanted.* London: Piatkus, 2012.

37 Leaf, Caroline. *Switch on Your Brain: The Key to Peak Happiness, Thinking, and Health.* BAKER Book House, 2018.

38 Leahy, Robert L. *The Worry Cure: Seven Steps to Stop Worry from Stopping You.* New York: Harmony Books, 2005.

39 Borkovec, Thomas & Hazlett-Stevens, Holly & Diaz, M.L.. (1999). The Role of Positive Beliefs about Worry in Generalized Anxiety Disorder and its Treatment. Clinical Psychology & Psychotherapy. 6. 126 - 138. 10.1002/(SICI)1099-0879(199905)6:2<126::AID-CPP193>3.0.CO;2-M.

Chapter Six

40 "How Much Are We Really Attached to Our Phones Physically, Cognitively..." Accessed March 17, 2023. https://pages.dscout.com/hubfs/downloads/dscout_mobile_touches_study_2016.pdf.

41 Girela-Serrano, Braulio M., Alexander D. Spiers, Liu Ruotong, Shivani Gangadia, Mireille B. Toledano, and Martina Di Simplicio. "Impact of Mobile Phones and Wireless Devices Use on Children and Adolescents' Mental Health: A Systematic Review." *European Child & Adolescent Psychiatry* (2022).

42 Madhav, K C, Shardulendra Prasad Sherchand, and Samendra Sherchan. "Association between Screen Time and Depression Among US Adults." Preventive medicine reports. U.S. National Library of Medicine, August 16, 2017. https://www.ncbi.nlm.nih.gov/pmc/articles/PMC5574844/.

43 Hoge, Elizabeth A., Eric Bui, Mihriye Mete, Samantha R. Philip, Caroline Gabriel, Meredith J. Ward, Rebecca Suzuki, Mary Ann Dutton, and Naomi M. Simon. "Treatment for Anxiety: Mindfulness Meditation versus Escitalopram (Tame): Design of a Randomized, Controlled Non-Inferiority Trial." *Contemporary Clinical Trials* 91 (2020): 105965. https://doi.org/10.1016/j.cct.2020.105965.

44 Pascal, Blaise, 1623-1662. Pascal's Pensées. New York :E.P. Dutton, 1958.

45 Ruth Haley Barton and Dallas Willard, *Invitation to Solitude and Silence: Experiencing God's Transforming Presence,* Expanded edition. (Downers Grove, Ill: IVP Books, 2010).

Chapter Seven

46 Rowland, David L., and Jacques J. van Lankveld. "Anxiety and Performance in Sex, Sport, and Stage: Identifying Common Ground." Frontiers in Psychology 10 (2019). https://doi.org/10.3389/fpsyg.2019.01615.

47 Schad, Tom. "Lindsey Vonn Talks Mental Health, Strain of Olympics: 'Honestly, Everyone Should Have a Therapist'." USA Today. Gannett Satellite Information Network, June 24, 2021. https://www.usatoday.com/story/sports/olympics/2021/06/24/lindsey-vonn-mental-health-strain-olympics-2022-beijing-games/5320659001/.

48 Gordon, Grant. "Cowboys QB Dak Prescott Talks Openly on Mental Health." NFL.com. NFL, September 11, 2020. https://www.nfl.com/news/cowboys-qb-dak-prescott-talks-openly-on-mental-health.

49 Herman, J. (2007, March 10) Shattered shame states and their repair. Lecture for The John Bowlby Memorial Lecture at Harvard Medical School, Department of Psychiatry, Victims of Violence Program, Somerville, MA 02143.

50 Kim S, Thibodeau R, & Jorgensen R (2011). Shame, guilt, and depressive symptoms: A meta-analytic review. Psychological Bulletin, 137, 68–96. 10.1037/a0021466

51 Sue, D. W., & Sue, D. (2016). Counseling the culturally diverse: theory and practice. 7th edition. Hoboken, New Jersey, John Wiley & Sons, Inc.

52 Warren, Rick. *The Purpose Driven Life: What on Earth Am I Here for?* Grand Rapids, MI: Zondervan, 2021.